Planning, Conducting, & Evaluating Workshops

A PRACTITIONER'S GUIDE TO ADULT EDUCATION

LEARNING
CONCEPTS

PLANNING, CONDUCTING, & EVALUATING

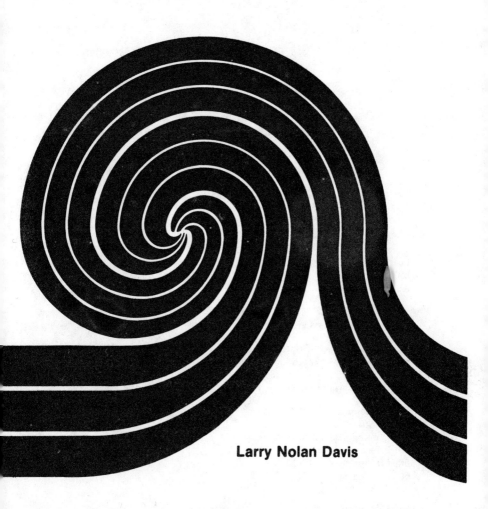

Larry Nolan Davis

WORKSHOPS

Learning Concepts, Inc.
2501 North Lamar
Austin, Texas 78705

1st Printing January 1975
2nd Printing May 1975
3rd Printing September 1975
4th Printing February 1976
5th Printing August 1977
6th Printing August 1978
7th Printing May 1979

Library of Congress Catalogue No. 74-82809

Edited and Designed by Barbara Gibbs

This book is dedicated—

> To Diane, whose life joined with mine yields ever new opportunities for learning.

> To Fred, a friend always with whom I can relax from learning.

> To my parents, who gave me tools for learning and the confidence to use them.

> To Johney Smith, my partner, with whom I worked out many of the following ideas in the practice of helping adults learn.

> And to Joe Rubio, who started me down the path that led to this book.

CONTENTS

AIDS

PUBLISHER'S FOREWORD

Learning Concepts, Inc. is pleased to present *Planning, Conducting, and Evaluating Workshops.* It represents an important contribution to our objective of publishing materials that translate social science theory for practical use in a variety of institutional settings. We feel the book is a significant new resource for the practicing adult educator.

Larry Davis's expertise in adult education combines a strong grasp of theory and broad experience in public and private organizations. As the author, he has drawn on this background to achieve an appropriate mix of theory and practical guidance in a usable format and an entertaining style. Dr. Earl McCallon collaborated in the book's design and development by suggesting applications for educational settings and served as a contributing editor.

Ray Bard
Publisher

PREFACE

BACKGROUND

Not long ago, historically speaking, children were people who read comic books and went to school. Adults were people who worked and looked after children. The arrangement seemed to work fairly well; the species survived, even flourished; and *Progress* was made. And made! And Made!

That presented a problem. To be sure, children still read "Superman" and went to school. Adults still wiped runny noses and worked. But it was noted that the adults looked a little uncertain, as if they did not know what to think of *Progress* or how to tell children about it.

"Let's hold a conference," someone suggested. And they did. Or rather they held thousands. From far and near adults gathered to talk over *Progress*, to share ideas, and to make merry. A few of them even went back to the Big School on the Hill to hear what the Esteemed Elders had to say.

For a time this seemed to help. Adults were seen to smile and walk firmly on the earth again. Then came new *Progress*, even bigger than before. A great cry was heard across the land. Adults—short and tall, female and male, white-clad and blue-clad—all looked at their outmoded tools in despair. It was clear that merely talking about *Progress* was not enough. Meanwhile, children had taken to reading *Mad* and watching astronauts and assassinations on television.

As we all know, however, man is not made for defeat. "I will learn to work with *Progress*," he said, "and I will learn how to instruct the children in its uses." From this resolve came multitudes of clinics, institutes, seminars, special interest groups, demonstrations, laboratories, workshops, and other exotic-sounding things.

So nowadays children are people who go to school and long for a hero like the one in the movie *Billy Jack*. Adults are people who work, look after children, and also long for a *Billy Jack*, while they learn to cope with *Progress* through workshops.

THE SCENE

Adult education is assuming increasing importance in the function of modern industrial societies. Within the last ten years recognition of its importance has increased dramatically. Today it has become almost axiomatic that continuing education is essential in meeting the needs of modern adults and of the organizations with which they work. Learning activities occupy more and more adult time, and the demand is still growing. Given this period of rapid growth, the practice of adult education has been highly experimental and the results have varied widely. The time has come, however, to begin the task of consolidation, to establish a discipline that has both order and consistency and that leads to predictable results. This book is offered as a step in that direction.

The fact that relatively similar adult learning activities bear a wide variety of labels causes a certain amount of confusion. In this book I am using the word *workshop* to encompass all those learning activities that occur in

4

group settings. A workshop, then, is any group meeting that has adult learning as a *primary* purpose. If no learning purpose exists, it is some other kind of meeting: a bridge party, lynch mob, or perhaps a political convention.

WHO'S IN CHARGE HERE?

In large part, modern adult education falls outside the realm of formal educational institutions. Its practitioners, the adult educators, are largely nonacademic. Titles such as staff-developer, inservice trainer, training director, facilitator, and human resource developer are appearing in many organizations. To varying degrees the people who work under these titles have received specialized training in preparation for this work. The bulk of adult education, however, is being undertaken by men and women who have received little or no special preparation, and who, having other full-time vocations, do not think of themselves particularly as adult educators. They are commonly school principals, personnel directors, program chairmen of various service and religious organizations, supervisors, union leaders, counselors, or simply workers in the wide variety of human organizations that make up a modern industrial society. Often they have been recruited for the task of adult education as an activity in addition to their regular duties. This doubling of roles results partially from a lack of funds to support full-time adult educators. It also results from the recognition that those closest to the need in time, space, and experience will quite often do the best job. This book shares that recognition.

So who's in charge here? For the most part you are, along with other men and women just like you. Desks piled sky-high under the pressures of other duties, you are taking the additional time and energy to plan, conduct, and evaluate workshops for the benefit of fellow adults. Properly, then, you deserve the title of adult educator, and this book is designed to assist you in those activities.

NEED FOR THIS BOOK

As I helped fellow adult educators develop skills for working with workshops, the need for a basic, concise, and complete guide to the theory and practice of adult education became clear. It was particularly needed since most practitioners had neither the time nor inclination to enter specialized and continuing training to develop these skills. Even experienced adult educators indicated the need for a handbook organized in a fashion that would make it usable as a reference in the midst of educational activities.

There are many good books on the subject. But for the most part they are both too long and too detailed to be considered basic. On the other hand, the basic ones are either incomplete, poorly organized (as in potpourri or hodgepodge), or polarized around one theory of learning to the exclusion of all others.

THE OBJECTIVES OF THIS BOOK

My first objective for the book is that it be a practical aid for those of you who are part-time adult educators with limited preparation for the job. Consequently I assume no specialized prerequisite skills on your part, other than the basic human ones that undoubtedly got you the job in the first place. In the course of the book I present a systematic approach for working with workshops, one that is both basic and complete. As

6

background I include "snapshots" of the theoretical war-fare in the field of adult education, but I also present a theoretical framework that will easily communicate from my experience to yours. Additionally I attempt to describe sufficient methods and tools to enable the book to stand on its own without further complexity.

My second objective for the book is that it serve as a useful reference and that it provide new insights for those of you who are experienced adult educators. To this end I present a sequence of chapters organized chronologically according to task, making it readily us-able in the rush of events. I describe the various learning theories within a framework that provides for easy (and perhaps irreverent) comparisons and explore their appli-cation to the practice of adult education. I attempt finally to demystify certain trade procedures, level some of the esoteric verbiage, blow through the smoke screens laid down by several specialized sects, and in general hack away at the proliferating underbrush of methods, techniques, and procedures by simply demonstrating their commonality, similarity, or sameness. In short, I attempt to achieve a purity worthy of any true discipline.

Fortunately achieving one objective achieves the other, since much of what appears complex in adult edu-cation is really only confusion resulting from the lack of a common language. As to that portion of adult educa-tion that really is complex, this book does not attempt to plumb the depths nor agonize over the nuances; it simply offers itself as a new tool to assist you in bringing quality to your workshops.

THE STRUCTURE

Basically the book contains an introduction and three major sections: "Planning Workshops," "Conducting Workshops," and "Evaluating Workshops." The introduction is an overview of adult learning theory complete with my own version of the same. The planning and conducting sections begin with short prefaces and are followed by separate chapters for the various procedures that fall under them. Each chapter begins with a short description of what one is "trying to get" from the procedure, followed where applicable by suggested tools, models, and methods. For the sake of coherence, the evaluation section is presented as an unbroken essay. As nearly as possible the arrangement of sections and chapters represents a chronological sequence of activities.

Included at certain points of the text are a series of worksheets which you may find useful in accomplishing the tasks required of you as an adult educator. When completed and assembled, these worksheets constitute the "Workshop Staff Packet" which contains all the data needed by you and other staff in carrying out the various workshop activities.

Following the section on evaluation is an aid "Further Resources" which lists a number of books and other resources that you may want to explore in further developing your skills as an adult educator. Footnote references found in the text refer to this section.

The book concludes with "The Manager's Guide to Adult Education" which summarizes much of the material contained in the body of the book and describes specific roles required of the manager in supporting adult learning activities. It is offered for your use in briefing your bosses and in gaining their assistance and support.

HOW THE BOOK MAY BE USED

As a result of this design I hope that you will be able to read quickly through the narrative sections in sequence, skimming over the methods, models, tools, and worksheets and coming back to them only when they may be put to work. In order to facilitate this kind of usage, I have made a determined effort to avoid the temptation of learned footnotes. As an additional convenience, the portion devoted to educational methods is edged in black so that you can locate it quickly at those crucial times when you decide that you must change your methods.

This is your book. Feel free to argue with it, change it, enjoy it, and build on it. The worksheets are included for a purpose; permission is hereby granted to copy them. Your use will prove my success in meeting the objectives for this book. May it serve you well.

INTRODUCTION

Working With Adult Learning

WHOM DO YOU SERVE?

Since many of you were recruited for this job, you obviously serve the person or organization who recruited you. In this work few of us are entirely our own bosses. Organizations, whether for profit, service, or fun, have purposes. As a result they also have needs. One of those needs is for the individuals within them to engage effectively in activities that lead toward accomplishing the organization's purposes. That's where you come in. One of your tasks is *to help individuals develop abilities that serve the organization's purposes.*

Individuals, however, have the strange habit of at least seeming to make some of their own choices. That means that they do not always do as told and that they do not always choose to learn what they should. Individuals have their own purposes and needs, and not all of them are met by any one organization. At the very least your task is to serve the individual's needs to the degree that he will choose to learn what the organization wants him to learn.

In a democratic society, most of us go a good deal further. We serve individual needs because individuals are important in themselves. Consequently we find ourselves helping individuals develop knowledge and abilities that serve their own purposes, including but not limited to those that get them the sought-after rewards from the organization.

As adult educators we have needs and purposes of our own. When we take on the job of serving individual and organizational needs, we are at the very same time attempting to serve our own. Unfortunately that often presents problems. Conflicts between any and all of these needs can and often do arise. In such instances we must rely on our skills for negotiation or remove ourselves from the conflict. This book is devoted to helping you develop the skills needed to avoid the conflicts inherent in serving three distinct sets of needs.

> ASIDE: Some writers in the field would have you serve the needs and purposes of society as well, but since I have found little agreement as to what they are, I simply suggest that you follow the dictates of your own biases, which ultimately means serving your own needs.

SETTING

It is said that everybody has to be somewhere. Bending that just a bit, we could say that everybody who participates in a workshop comes from somewhere. Later we will take a look at the setting of the workshop itself, but at this point we are concerned with the setting from which the participant comes.

For the most part, adult learners come from and are sponsored by organizations. They come from particular places within those organizations with particular bosses, peers, or subordinates. Those particular places have certain ways of doing things and certain attitudes. To put it simply, workshop participants do not come from "nowhere"; they come from and return to particular places with particular *operational styles*.

14

ASIDE: In the fairly rare event of participants representing only themselves, they still have to go back home to family and friends.

Let's take a look at some of these styles. There is a great deal written about them in both the literature of management and group dynamics. Such terms as *autocratic, humanistic,* and *paternalistic* crop up. There are various schemes for analyzing styles such as the "X-Y Theory" and the "Management Grid." There are also a few strategies for neutralizing their effects, "Management by Objectives" being perhaps the best known.

For our purposes a look at three styles should suffice. These are drawn from the study of leadership in groups, but they may also be used to describe management and organizational styles. At one extreme is the *authoritarian* style; at the other is *laissez faire*; and in between we find the *democratic* style.

authoritarian	democratic	laissez faire
▲	▲	▲

Perhaps a brief description of each would help:

Authoritarian—as in bosses, drill sergeants, and certain teachers.

Democratic—as in majority rule, participation, and apple pie.

Laissez faire—as in "let it all hang out," "do your own thing," or "let things take their course."

15

Let me hasten to say that no one of these is either good or bad in itself. Each will work, and each has a place given the realities of this world.

These styles are worthy of far more serious treatment, but the point is for you to be aware of the range of styles and their effects on the participants in your workshops. Participants are influenced before, during, and after your workshop by the dominant style "back in the shop." If the style of your workshop is radically different from the style there, serious problems may arise. Let's take a look at some workshop styles and the theories from which they arise.

THEORETICAL WARFARE

Warring parties

The field of learning theory in general and adult learning theory in particular can be likened to a battleground. There is a confusing array of uniforms, and to make matters worse, it looks rather like a free-for-all. Connectionists, interactionists, cognitivists, humanists, behaviorists, pragmatists, functionalists, gestaltists, conditioners, and reinforcers are milling about and appear to be shooting in all directions. Shifting alliances, turncoating, and double-agentry are all alleged. Given such a state of affairs, perhaps a little irreverent war analysis is not out of place.

It appears that the conflict centers mainly around that old argument regarding man's free will or lack of it. On one side there are the *determinists* and on the other the *freewillers*. Both sides demand unconditional allegiance and loyalty. In the middle are a few *neutralists*, under fire from both sides. No one appears to have a clear advantage, and the dispute seems no closer to being settled than it did when we were kids.

Tactical skirmishes

A highlight of this war is the adroit use of tactical maneuvering. To a casual observer, the skirmishes centering around the definitions for "theory" and "learning" might appear to be mere saber-rattling. A closer inspection reveals skillful maneuvering for position and strength testing.

Drawing the battle lines

The major engagements center around two questions: "How does learning occur?" and "How should one teach?" From the determinists, one hears assertions that learning involves establishing a connection between a stimulus and a response or some variations along that line. Man is essentially determined—a passive switchboard. Teaching strategies range from manipulating the stimulus to rewarding the response, with variations in the time and method of reward.

At the other extreme, the freewillers are not too interested in the mechanics of learning but are considerably interested in the requisite conditions, the most important of which is man himself—an active organism, the source of his own responses. Teaching strategies involve creating climates for learning, assisting the learner in his own quest, and facilitating the (natural) learning process.

In the middle, the neutralists either agree with both or reserve judgement. Or they risk the assertion that the organism may have something to do with selecting certain of the stimuli to which it will respond and with regulating both intensity and kind of response.

Since all sides show some success with their theories, and since none have been able to annihilate the

17

others, the battle is likely to continue for a good long time.

Casualties

Here is the curious part: I have seen no casualties on this battlefield. Since the battle is purely theoretical, no one gets hurt.

In the peaceful day-in-day-out practitioner's field, however, casualties are strewn all about, and I have seen no one fighting. As a result of unquestioned educational practices, individuals move like robots through their tasks or wander the streets in an idle, simian haze; organizations efficiently destroy the resources that feed them or sputter along in endless circles of individual incompetence; and educators (authoritarian, democratic, and laissez faire) turn to pillars of salt from looking back and wondering what went wrong.

A tentative proposal for peace

If there is a resolution to the theoretical warfare in learning theory, it lies in the direction indicated by Teilhard de Chardin. In *The Phenomenon of Man* Chardin offers an explanation that at least by implication encompasses and unifies these various theories. As he sees it, there is a "within" and a "without" to all things. The without is made up of *tangential* (physical) energy, the focus of scientific inquiry as we now know it. Tangential energy is subject to the laws, theories, and measurements of science. The within is made up of *radial* energy, the energy of knowing, which at present reaches its apex in man's reflective thought. Somehow these two energies are bound and related: "To think, we must eat. But what a variety of thoughts we get out of one slice of bread!"[1]

18

Determinists and freewillers alike have perhaps given an accurate account of reality, but they have described different levels of it. Harmony in the field of learning theory may come from the recognition that there is more than one level of reality.

If this peace proposal is to bear fruit, however, there must be some fighting in the practitioner's field. Most of the current casualties appear to result from educators (knowingly or not) embracing one theory to the exclusion of the others and religiously adopting its teaching style (authoritarian, democratic, or laissez faire), whether or not it is appropriate to the situation. As a means of combating this, I propose below my adult learning "theory," and in the remainder of the book, a teaching strategy that follows from it.

MY ADULT LEARNING THEORY

Shortcomings:
1. It is not scientific.
2. It is not concise.
3. It is not internally consistent.

Good points:
1. It comes from my experience.
2. It can be validated by your experience.
3. It is open-ended.
4. It allows for flexibility of style in meeting needs of adult learners.
5. It does not demand loyalty.

In this context, *adult* does not necessarily mean a person eighteen years of age or older. It refers partly to a stage of skill development which falls somewhere between learning how to talk and dying. It refers to a person whose knowledge is based to some degree on first-hand experience.

19

The following theory does not refer to some ideal adult, but to a person who is changing and to the process and direction of that change. *Adultness,* as used in this book, refers to a level of maturity, regardless of a person's age.

Essentially, my adult learning theory is a set of declarative statements based on experience. You may place question marks after some statements and ignore others. You may add statements of your own; you may delete others. No single statement is essential. My experience is different from yours.

Adults and Effective Workshops

1. *Adults are people who have a good deal of first hand experience.* Some have reflected on their experience and learned from it. Some have not. Others have changed their behavior without reflecting on their experience, their words and actions are at odds. Most have learned by experience that their powers are limited; no longer do they expect the sand fort to hold back the sea.

   Effective workshops tap participants' experience as a major resource for learning. Effective workshops are a source of new experience for participants. Effective workshops help adults convert experience into learning.

2. *Adults are people who have relatively large bodies subject to the stress of gravitational stimuli.* When they were younger, many adults slept comfortably on hardwood floors. When they are older the floor is not so comfortable. Most experience discomfort when they sit too long in hard chairs. Chairs that are too short or too narrow are worse. Some adults fall asleep in chairs that are just right.

Effective workshops have effective chairs or a good many coffee breaks.

3. *Adults are people who have set habits and strong tastes.* Many adults need coffee in the morning; some in the afternoon. Some hate coffee and get their caffeine from cokes or tea. Some would never touch caffeine, preferring health drinks instead. Some need to smoke; some insist on no smoking. Some like spicy language; some are offended by profanity. All find learning difficult when their habits and tastes are violated.

   Effective workshops are sensitive to adult habits and tastes and accommodate as many as possible.

4. *Adults are people who have some amount of pride.* Although some are dependent much of the time, all adults like to think of themselves as independent some of the time. In military training the strong emphasis on destroying independent judgement is strong proof that independence exists.

   Workshops can be used to destroy independence and create people who obey. Effective workshops develop greater abilities in self-direction and responsibility.

5. *Adults are people with very tangible things to lose.* Effective workshops are concerned with gain, not with proving inadequacy. Effective workshops aim for one hundred percent success.

6. *Adults are people who have developed a reflex toward authority.* Some buck it. Some bow to it. Some relate to it as a resource. And some just let it pass. When adults become their own authorities, learning power (radial energy) progresses geometrically.

21

Effective workshops make appropriate use of authority.

7. *Adults are people who have decisions to make and problems to solve.* Many have the nostalgic idea of returning to school, of participating in pure learning. Few of them do. Instead they go to movies or watch T.V. When they do go for learning, most are seeking help in solving problems or making decisions.

   Effective workshops tend to be both problem-centered and entertaining.

8. *Adults are people who have a great many preoccupations outside of a particular learning situation.* People are animals who have unusual difficulty in focusing. Most adults have heavy demands on their time, greater on some occasions than on others. Most have very real life commitments. Some adults are organized, some impatient, some overwhelmed.

   Effective workshops are sensitive to their space in the adult world; they are not hoggish. Effective workshops achieve a balance between tight presentation and the time needed for learning integration.

9. *Modern adults are people who are bewildered by their options.* Effective workshops assist them in selection.

10. *Adults are people who have developed group behaviors consistent with their needs.* Some are hostile, some helpful. Some are aggressive, some passive. Some are defensive, some open. Most adults select from a range of ready behaviors the one that seems best calculated to meet their needs in a given situation.

All have needs. All attempt to have those needs met by the group. Some are more successful than others. All are successful to the degree allowed by the group. All behaviors are reciprocal. Some behaviors help the group, others hinder it.

Effective workshops concern themselves with the needs of their participants. Effective workshops attempt to meet those needs in ways that are helpful to the group. Effective workshops are a blending of many kinds of behavior.

11. *Adults are people who have established emotional frameworks consisting of values, attitudes, and tendencies.* All need emotional frameworks for successful functioning. Some function successfully with their framework; others do not. Some are aware of most of their framework. Most are aware of only some of it.

Progress produces pressure for change. Some change is life-giving. Some change leads to despair. All change is disorienting. Too much change in too short a time is destructive. The ability to change is directly proportional to the degree of safety adults feel. Rhetoric and argument do not produce change in the emotional framework. New experience may. Values are the hardest to change. Emotional change does not necessarily produce behavior change; behavior change does not necessarily require attitude change.

Effective workshops assist adults in making behavior changes. Effective workshops assist adults in becoming more competent. Effective workshops may assist adults in making changes in their emotional frameworks when there is a high degree of safety, mutual commitment, and choice.

23

12. *Adults are people who have developed selective stimuli filters.* People have at least five sensing systems. These systems are interrelated. Stimuli bombard these interrelated systems. An experience is composed of at least one stimulus. It is difficult to isolate a stimulus. Most experiences are composed of numerous stimuli. An environment is a space that is experienced. Environments contain countless stimuli.

    People respond to stimuli by "filtering" those which are distressing, unpleasant, etc. In short, most adults hear what they want to hear.

    Effective workshops exert some control over stimuli. Effective workshops focus on more than one sensing system. Effective workshops penetrate the filters.

13. *Adults are people who respond to reinforcements.* Most respond favorably to positive reinforcement most of the time. All require negative reinforcement some of the time. Some require reinforcement more often than others. Some reinforcements are insulting. Most reinforcement loses effect with senseless repetition.

    Effective workshops are built on *appropriate* reinforcement.

14. *Adults are people who need a vacation.* All good adult educators know this, and effective workshops accommodate it.

15. *Adults are people who are supposed to appear in control and who therefore display restricted emotional response.* Many have long lost children locked up inside them. The children may be delightful or they may be horrid.

24

Workshops are often environments in which the doors come unlocked. Effective workshops do not add to the bars, neither do they pry open the doors. Effective workshops are prepared for emotional release if it occurs.

16. *Adults are people who have strong feelings about learning situations.* Everybody comes from somewhere. That somewhere was either a good experience or a bad one. In it they either succeeded or failed. As a result, most people have strong tendencies toward competition, cooperation, or withdrawal. Most can develop good feelings about learning situations.

    Effective workshops are filled with success experiences.

17. *Modern adults are people who are secretly afraid of falling behind and being replaced.* Effective workshops allow them to keep pace and grow with confidence.

18. *Adults are people who can skip certain basics.* If they are about to build a footbridge, adults may learn only the mathematical principles required to build it. For adults, foundations for the future are often irrelevant and unnecessary; the future is now.

    Effective workshops are not bound to basics. Effective workshops get on with helping adults learn to cope with present problems. Effective workshops are little concerned with remedial education.

19. *Adults are people who more than once find the foundations of their lives stripped away.* The college dorm is not the same as the room back home. Leisurely afternoons are burned away by the newborn

baby. Jobs are lost. Parents die. Ideals are tarnished. Divorces occur. Bodies don't perform as they once did. Children leave home. The stock market crashes. Responsibilities are taken away. Retirement becomes mandatory. Mates die and leave them alone.

Effective workshops go beyond helping adults cope; they help them learn to live again.

20. *Adults are people who can change.* This is the prime tenet of faith for effective workshops.

21. *Adults are people who have a past.* Their memories are filled with regrets, guilts, and nostalgia for magic times. A few are blessed with accurate memories. A few are blessed with insight.

    Effective workshops are concerned with developing new competencies; the "why's" of the past are someone else's concern.

22. *Adults are people who have ideas to contribute.* Effective books are those that leave room for them. Therefore . . .

23.

A SYSTEMATIC APPROACH TO WORKSHOPS

The adult education system offered in this book, unlike the theory, is both concise and complete. It, too, is drawn from experience. And when followed, it leads to successful workshops. Below is an outline of the major activities and procedures involved in workshops. It is also an outline of the remainder of this book. Again, the arrangement as nearly as possible represents a chronological sequence of activities.

    I. Planning the Workshop
- A. Assessing needs
- B. Specifying objectives
- C. Selecting resources
- D. Designing activities
- E. Budgeting
- F. Making arrangements
- G. Rehearsing
- H. Packing

    II. Conducting the Workshop
- A. Setting up
- B. Setting the learning climate
- C. Agreeing on objectives
- D. Directing learning activities
- E. Closing shop

    III. Evaluating the Workshop

PART I

Planning The Workshop

PLANNING

When the word *planning* comes up in a book like this, many people grow uneasy. For some it simply means a lot of busy work when what we need to do is "get in there and get the job done." (Have you ever helped someone move who was using that method?) For others it means the tedious task of racking the brain trying to anticipate all possible problems. For others it produces an anxiety about the event, and for a rare few it represents a curb on spontaneity. But for most people, planning in a technical book like this apparently means something different from what it means when it is used in a household phrase such as "planning a party." That is probably because so many books follow the word with a great many unreadable charts and graphs.

In this book the word is used as in "planning a party." Here is my simple checklist for planning:

A complete plan (of any kind) contains a specification of the *Five W's and the H.*

W_1—specifies *why*, a statement of interest, tendency, documented need, or pure whim.

W_2—specifies *what* you will be doing or trying to do, often known as an objective.

W_3—specifies both *who* and to *whom.*

W_4—specifies *when* you will start doing it and *when* you hope to stop.

W_5—specifies *where.*

31

H —specifies *how*; the strategy or flow of events that lead to the *what*.

This is not a method for planning, nor is it a format for the plan. It is a checklist, a tool for checking any plan or piece of a plan for completeness.

In the eight chapters of this section, I have provided methods and formats intended to help you in specifying the *Five W's and the H*. Try them in the order presented, and you will end with a planned workshop.

Chapter 1: Assessing Needs—a guide to specifying **why.**

Chapter 2: Specifying Objectives—a guide to specifying **what.**

Chapter 3: Selecting Resources—a guide to specifying **who** and some of **how.**

Chapter 4: Designing Activities—a guide to specifying most of the **how** and a good portion of **when.**

Chapter 5: Budgeting—budgeting is not an essential part of every complete plan, but is included here as the how of **how.**

Chapter 6: Making Arrangements—a guide to specifying **where**, with some implications from how and for when.

Chapter 7: Rehearsing—a guide to refining all the above.

Chapter 8: Packing—a guide without which **what** might never be reached.

Finally, let's consider the relationship between comprehensive planning and spontaneity. Too often planning *is* a curb on spontaneity. The plan becomes the objective rather than a means of reaching it. This is typified by the planner who gets flustered when things get off course, or the planner who sees participants as prisoners who must march exactly to his scheduled drumbeats.

The other extreme is the person who, in the name of spontaneity, uses the take-things-as-they-come method. In practice this often translates to "blow it off," "take it easy," or "it will become clear as we go along," further translated to mean, "I ain't taking no responsibility. It's your problem."

A good plan is one that allows you to relax, knowing that all the bases are covered and still leaves room for spontaneity and change.

ASSESSING NEEDS

1

Assessing learning needs is perhaps the most difficult and important part of the adult educator's job. If no learning need can be found, there should be no workshop. Learning needs are found in two places: in problems and in opportunities. In his book *Training by Objectives* Odiorne defines a problem as "a deviation from a standard, important enough to be solved, and to which somebody will be committed to a solution."[2] For learning purposes, the standard involved is the desired or required behavior; a deviation represents the present behavior; and the learning need is the difference between the two. *Important enough to be solved* implies priority setting based on the degree of the problem's effect. *To which somebody will be committed* means simply that if no one cares to change the behavior, it won't be changed. Extending this thought, an opportunity might be defined as A NEW STANDARD IMPORTANT ENOUGH TO BE ATTEMPTED AND INTERESTING ENOUGH TO TRIGGER A DEFINITE COMMITMENT.

Assessing needs serves at least four purposes:

1. It gives a place to begin.
2. It provides a direction.
3. It answers the question "Why?"
4. It authorizes continuation or gives permission to stop.

35

In the literature regarding needs assessment, two polar positions have emerged. For the sake of consistency I call one *authoritarian* and the other *laissez faire*. On the authoritarian side needs assessment is an activity entered into by the educator in behalf of his participants and with the blessing of the organization (where applicable). Ideally the authoritarian side moves organizations and individuals toward new standards of insight and behavior, but often it simply teaches them what they "ought to know." On the laissez faire extreme, needs assessment is an activity entered into by the educator in which he is the passive recipient of individual needs. Ideally the laissez faire side allows individuals to grow to new levels of self-direction, presumably in behalf of their organizations; but often it merely gives them "what they want."

Moving a notch from the authoritarian extreme to a position called *moderate authoritarian*, needs assessment would additionally involve supervisors and management. The *moderate laissez faire* position would call for an actively involved educator.

In the *democratic* position, needs assessment is an activity entered into by an active educator in collaboration with participants and management. The democratic position moves individuals and organizations to mutually agreeable insights and behaviors, but it can lead to polarization, dissension, and disruption.

These five positions may be schematically illustrated as follows:

NEEDS ASSESSMENT
In an Organizational Context

Authoritarian	Democratic	Laissez faire
*Educator	*Management	*Self-directed
*Arbitrary authority	*Individual	individuals
	*Active educator	*Passive educator
	*Mutual agreement	

Moderate-authoritarian	Moderate-laissez faire
*Management	*Individuals
*Educator (active	*Active educator
or passive)	

When participants represent only themselves and no organization is involved, we are left with the following three positions:

Voluntary Individual Participation

Authoritarian	Democratic	Laissez faire
*Educator	*Individual	*Self-directed
*Arbitrary authority	*Active Educator	individuals
	*Mutual Agreement	*Passive educator

Perhaps the importance of needs assessment will become clearer if we consider a few real life situations that typically produce learning needs. Following are two lists, one for individuals and one for organizations.

Situations Affecting Individuals:

A new job
An old job with new duties
Loss of job
New community responsibilities
New hobbies
Marriage
Children
Adolescent children
Separation from children
Middle age
Retirement
Old age
A changing world
Aloneness

Situations Affecting Organizations:

A new organization is formed.
A new person joins the organization.
A present employee (or member) takes new job.
Progress leads to new methods for old jobs.
New tools and equipment are added.
Conflicts arise within the organization.
Changes are made in purpose, policy, or structure.
A changing world requires organizational change.
Organizational decline sets in.

There are two major methods for needs assessment: the Problem Analysis Method and the Competency Model Method. Other methods are apparently variations of these two. Following is a full description of each, complete with suggestions for application.

A discussion of authoritarian, laissez faire, and democratic applications is included to assist you in making a choice of style appropriate to the organizations with which you work.

In addition, you will find discussion of a *simplified needs assessment* for use under certain limiting circumstances; and a discussion of alternatives to be considered when group size, available time, or distance from the participants becomes a problem.

To assist you in conducting a needs assessment, two worksheets are included, one for the Problem Analysis Method and one for the Competency Model Method. When completed, these worksheets may be added to the others to compose a *Workshop Staff Packet*. Again, permission to copy the worksheets is granted.

THE PROBLEM ANALYSIS METHOD

With this method a problem statement is the starting point, followed by a systematic process of moving from the problem statement to a series of learning needs that are then ranked in order of priority. It has both individual and organizational uses.

Process Steps

1. Stating the problem(s)
2. Refining the problem statement
3. Supporting the problem statement
4. Finding the needs
5. Separating learning from nonlearning needs
6. Assigning priorities
7. Testing commitment

Process Description

1. Stating the Problem(s)

A problem (or perhaps more than one) is stated. We then probe to see if it is really the statement of a problem. There is a common human tendency to state a solution when a problem is called for.

Example: Question: "What is the problem?"
Solution: "They need motivation training."
Probe: "Why? What's happening? Describe it."
Problem: "They're always late for work."
(See *The Case of the Pokey Elevators*, p. 49.)

40

2. Refining the Problem Statement

In the step above, there is a correctly stated problem, but is it the problem you should attack? Often there is a more fundamental problem than the one initially stated. Continuing our previous example:

> Problem: "They're always late for work."
> Clarifying probe: "You mean they don't get their work done on time?"
> Denial: "Oh no. *We* always meet *our* deadlines!"
> Clarifying probe: "You mean they do sloppy work, then?"
> Denial: "Good Lord, no! *We* turn out the best work in the whole place!"
> Shift question: "Well then, what is the problem with their being late to work?"
> New problem: "My boss came through the shop at 8:00 sharp the other morning, and only two people were here."

Larger problems must often be broken into their component parts in order to work with them. The kind of probing demonstrated above may also be used for this purpose.

3. Supporting the Problem Statement

So far you have only a statement that someone has *called* a problem; you should make certain it isn't a crank call. There must be evidence to support the allegation. There are numerous ways to get this evidence. Here are a few of them.

    a. Ask how often the problem occurs.
    b. Ask for the specific examples or incidents.
    c. Have the situation role-played.
    d. Ask some other people.

e. Check organizational records and reports.
f. Ask how many people are affected.
g. Go see for yourself.

4. Finding the Needs

There is now a correctly stated problem apparently important enough to be solved. It is time to determine what *needs* to happen to solve it. Solutions often require several changes, and there are normally several possible change combinations. Exactly *who* needs to learn exactly what? Are new tools needed, new decisions required, structural modifications necessary? The process of arriving at a solution can range from selecting the best of several common sense proposals to constructing models of possible cause/effect chains and computer testing for feasibility

5. Separating Learning from Nonlearning Needs

The needs list must be divided into those needs that can be taken care of by someone learning something and those that have to be solved in some other way. The need for adequate equipment is not a learning need; the proper use of equipment is. Here are some more examples:

Learning Needs	*Nonlearning Needs*
decision making skills	need for a decision
use of forms	need for new forms
following directions	too many bosses
organizing work	too little time
communication skills	bottlenecks
safety habits	unsafe conditions
achieving objectives	lack of objectives
greater productivity	inadequate salary
etc.	etc.

42

The above needs are related and interdependent. Often the nonlearning needs should be met before or concurrently with the learning needs. New behaviors are not likely to last if the environment does not support them.

6. Assigning Priorities

You now have before you your potential tasks, but since there is seldom enough time and money to go around, they should be ranked in priority order. The pattern of changes contained in the solution may suggest the priorities.

7. Testing Commitment
Finally, you must know whether anybody is committed to the solution. This amounts to finding out if anyone will attend and if the top people in the organization will support the solution.

Suggestions for Applications

When working with groups in the Problem Analysis Method, brainstorming (a rapid-fire listing of problems without critique, see p. 134) is an effective technique for Step One. In the unlikely event that no one states a problem, you might begin with mini-cases (p. 137) or mini-role play (p. 142). These usually uncover some problems; if not, you have nothing more to do.

When working with organizations as a whole, starting with a simulation (p. 143) can be fun and lead to an active problem-stating session. A representative vertical cross section of the organization is required if it is impractical to involve the entire organization.

Advantages to Problem Analysis Method

- Groups may be either *ad hoc* or ongoing

- The educator may turn the data over to others to actually conduct the learning activities

- Requires little background in the indicated areas of learning need

- Leads to high learning motivation since learning activities are designed to solve immediate problems

- Leads to immediate satisfaction when problem is solved

Disadvantages to Problem Analysis Method

- Can lead to crisis planning

- Does not lead naturally to sequenced learning

- Does not reveal new opportunities for learning

- Does not provide a great deal of latitude for individual preferences or pacing

- Participants are often reluctant to admit that problems exist

Problem Analysis Worksheet

The following worksheet is provided for your use in recording the results of a problem analysis needs assessment. The title indicates that it becomes the first page of the *Workshop Staff Packet* when the workshop is based on the Problem Analysis Method of needs assessment. (If the Competency Model Method is used instead, then the alternate Worksheet One found later in this chapter becomes the first page of the packet.)

The space designated by the word *Group* is for describing the group (or groups) from which the data came. Each problem statement emerging from Step Three of the procedure should be entered in one of the spaces provided. Separate columns are provided for the learning and nonlearning needs that fall under each problem statement. If related, they may be listed across from each other. Smaller vertical columns are provided for the priority numbers. The number sequence may include all the needs on the worksheet, or the needs under each problem may be sequenced separately.

NEEDS ASSESSMENT: PROBLEM ANALYSIS

Group

PROBLEM (supported by data)

NEEDS:	Learning	Nonlearning
Priority #		Priority #

PROBLEM (supported by data)

NEEDS:	Learning	Nonlearning
Priority #		Priority #

PROBLEM (supported by data)

NEEDS:	Learning	Nonlearning
Priority #		Priority #

PROBLEM (supported by data)

NEEDS:	Learning	Nonlearning
Priority #		Priority #

47

I picked this story up on the circuit. I believe it was attributed to a book on operations research, but I was unable to find the text. I would therefore like to express my appreciation to the author, whoever he is, and my apologies for modifications that may have occurred in its transmission.

It is separated from the text so that you may conveniently use it in a problem-stating session.

THE CASE OF THE POKEY ELEVATORS

Once upon a time, a very responsible manager of a twenty-story office building in New York City was besieged by complaints from his tenants. "The elevators are too slow!" they complained in a chorus. Being a responsible manager, he immediately called an engineering firm to have a look at the problem. During a preliminary discussion this rough floor plan was drawn.

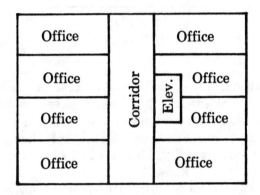

After an exhaustive study utilizing stop watches and traffice flow charts, the engineering firm gave him a proposal for the installation of two newer and faster elevators in the existing shafts. The price tag was $100,000 for an average time gain of 3.335 minutes from top to bottom for each elevator. This shaved an average of twenty seconds off the waiting time on each floor. "My, that's a lot of money," he said, "and twenty seconds is not a lot of time. I'll let you know."

Since he was also responsible to the building owners, he called another firm. After another exhaustive study, they made their proposal. What he should do, they said, was leave the present elevators alone and add two new elevators at the ends of the central corridor like this:

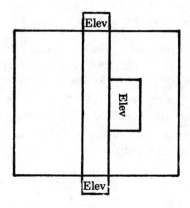

This solution, they said, would cost a little more, $150,000 to be precise, but would save tenants much more time, i.e., an average of 35 seconds shaved off the waiting time on each floor. "My, that should do the trick," he said uneasily, "but I will have to consult the owners. I'll let you know."

Now this is the sad part. He knew the owners would not spend that much, and the complaints were growing louder and more angry. In a fever he went to the Yellow Pages looking for someone to help him with his problem. His eyes skimmed down the page:

— "Probabilities"

— "Probers"

— "Problem Consultants"

"That's what I need," he said, "a problem consultant!" He quickly dialed the number.

Now this problem consultant was a strange dude. He practically went to sleep while the building manager described the problem. And for the next couple of days he wandered aimlessly through the building, doing nothing as far as the building manager could see. On the

50

third day he wandered into the manager's office and slouched into a chair.

"Well," he began, "you told me that your problem was slow elevators. What that said to me was that your solution to tenant complaints was faster elevators. But that wasn't really your problem. What those folks were trying to tell you is that they are bored stiff while waiting for the elevators. That's your real problem."

So for less than $1,000, mirrors were installed beside the elevators on every floor. Women straightened their hair, men their ties. There were no more complaints.

THE COMPETENCY MODEL METHOD

Developing a competency model (also known as a behavioral model) is the first step in this method. Subsequent steps lead to a specification of what needs to be learned to meet the standard of the model. The needs are then ranked in order of priority.

This method is not primarily concerned with what is wrong but with what is possible. As such it lends itself to the pursuit of new opportunities. Of the two methods it is perhaps the easier to work with. It has both individual and organizational uses.

Process Steps

1. Developing a Competency Model
2. Discovering Present Levels of Performance
3. Specifying Needs
4. Separating Learning from Non-learning Needs
5. Assigning Priorities
6. Testing Commitment

Process Description

1. Developing a Competency Model

Your first task is to develop a model for desirable or required competencies. As used here, *competency* means sufficient knowledge and ability to meet and succeed in the necessities of living. (Competencies are also called *behaviors*.) Such models range from the simple (one or two competencies required to perform a single task) to the complex (all the competencies required to fill a particular role or position).

In order to develop a model, you must clearly establish what behaviors are required. There are several ways to find out:

— consulting competent practitioners
— watching competent practitioners
— consulting relevant research
— conducting relevant research
— consulting supervisors
— reviewing job descriptions and performance standards
— conducting a task analysis
— asking prospective participants

Opportunities occasionally call for models never seen before. In that event, you are forced to make an informed guess about the competencies required and try them out. But since there is seldom anything entirely new under the sun, you would be wise to exhaust the above resources first.

In stating competencies there is a tendency to be overly general, to state slogans instead. For example:

Competency Model for Supervisors

Overly general slogans
{
1. Leadership

2. Dedication

3. Communication
}

Often these are simply incomplete descriptions. For the above examples we might seek answers to questions such as the following:

53

Leadership
- what "style(s)" of leadership?
- as demonstrated by what?

Dedication
- to what?
- to whom?
- as demonstrated by what?

Communication
- with whom?
- in what language?
- does this mean:
  - a. giving clear instructions?
  - b. giving effective instructions?
  - c. listening?
  - d. listening and hearing?
  - e. ability to give and receive criticism?
  - f. ability to reach agreement?

There is also a tendency to state vague qualities, rather than competencies:

Competency Model for Supervisors (cont.)

Vague qualities {
4. Good character

5. Patience

6. Motivation

7. Good appearance
}

This leads to several difficulties such as:

Who sets the standards?
How do you know they are being met?
How does one learn how to be that way?
Etc.

It also runs the danger of concealing biases about things such as short or long hair, short or long skirts, purple or green skin, etc.

Say What You Mean. It is a good practice to be as specific as possible in stating competencies. Specifying the real-life application seems to be helpful. Also the use of sentences complete with nouns, verbs, and modifiers is recommended. Let's try to say a portion of what might have been meant by "leadership."

Specific competency statements

1. A good line supervisor knows the three basic leadership "styles": authoritarian, democratic, and laissez faire.

2. A good line supervisor is competent in using all three styles.

3. A good line supervisor knows which style is appropriate to the specific employee and the specific situation.

These are only samples; they are not prescriptions. Different models call for different formats. They are based on my experience and are written in my style. You will develop your own. You should strive, however, to say what you mean, to say things that have meaning to others, and to say them as completely as possible.

2. Discovering Present Levels of Performance

In this step we are trying to discover just how prospective participants are doing in relation to the
model. There are several ways to go about it. Let's
look at a few of them.

Reviewing personnel evaluations may
provide some indication, but often
they are too vague and too general to
be of much use.

Reviewing reports may yield data on
behaviors in real life situations but
tend to gloss over the problems.

Asking supervisors can provide valuable information if the supervisor is
objective, observant, and willing to
level.

Testing participants is problematic
since most canned tests measure apti-
tude rather than behavior. Written
tests tend to measure reading, writing,
and parroting abilities. Tests may be
perceived as threatening or insulting.

Having participants try it is interesting. This usually takes the form of
having participants try out the behavior in a situation that simulates real
life conditions. Examples include case
studies, mini-cases, role plays, dry
runs, social simulations, etc. (see Me-

56

thods Primer, Chapter 4). This is, to be sure, a form of testing, but since it is closer to life there is usually less resistance. It is also a much better measure of present performance.

Observing participant behavior in real life situations is obviously the best measure. The difficulty lies in isolating a particular behavior for observation and in deciding whether inadequate behavior is due to a lack of competency or to other variables such as poor supervision. Most real life situations are too complex for this direct approach.

Asking participants may yield mixed results. Asking is not necessarily receiving; you may get a silly answer or none. Much depends on the level of trust established by the educator and by the environment. There are also difficulties in objectivity and precision. Still this method often yields the most valuable and accurate data when there is an adequate trust level and when there is an adequate format for the answer (see p. 66 for example format).

There are pitfalls in all these methods. Sometimes it is helpful to use more than one. Choose your method(s) to fit the situation, but whichever you choose, don't get hung up in a quest for precision. Present methodology is incapable of it. Besides, the focus here is on reaching the desired behavior, not on documenting deviation from it. Leave that to the academicians.

3. Specifying Needs

Once the present level of performance has been determined, your task is to describe what is needed for participants to reach the desired level of the model. This is made considerably easier if you have been specific in developing the model. Using the previous example of supervisory leadership competencies, assume that you discovered that a particular supervisor 1) knew the three basic leadership styles and 2) knew their appropriate uses. By the simple method of asking him, you also discovered that he felt uncomfortable in using the authoritarian style even when appropriate and was to that degree ineffective as a supervisor. His need *is to be able to use the authoritarian style effectively.*

4. Separating Learning from Nonlearning Needs

This step is not as essential as in the problem analysis method of needs assessment, but it occasionally serves a purpose. Continuing with the previous example, assume that upon further discussion with this particular supervisor you found that his discomfort came from two sources.

> A. His boss maintained an open-door policy. When the supervisor employed the authoritarian style, his boss undercut it by listening to and sympathizing with the complaints of certain employees.

B. Like most of us the supervisor wanted to be liked. Consequently his authoritarian style was limited to thin, hollow demands which, when ignored, led to outbursts of ineffectual anger.

In this case the open door problem is not a learning need for the supervisor. His weak authoritarian style is a learning need and suggests a learning experience in assertive behavior most likely employing role play. (The new behavior, however, is not likely to last if the boss doesn't close his door.)

Other situations might reveal the need for supportive management systems or for new and better tools, both nonlearning needs. Let me stress, however, that in using the competency model method you are not primarily concerned with the causes of inadequate behavior but with the specific learning required to reach the desirable behavior. Most often you can simply specify the difference and get on with the learning.

NOTE: If you failed to get rid of those vague qualities (good appearance, etc.) earlier, now is the time to toss them out, or you will find yourself in the untenable position of designing learning activities to try to reach them. (An exception might be made for stewardess training, but in that case good appearance would become specific things like acceptable hair styles, make-up, etc.)

5. Assigning Priorities

   The competency model method has the advantage of suggesting a logical learning sequence leading from simple to more complex behaviors. Obviously such a sequence has implications for priority setting.

   Also involved in assigning priorities are such factors as organizational needs, timing, relative cost, etc. These factors often rule out behavioral changes that are extremely difficult to achieve.

6. Testing Commitment

   Following the previous example, you must find out if the supervisor will attempt the learning and if his boss will support it. If they are only mildly interested in the change, then a fruitless workshop is likely to occur and it is better to abort the mission.

Suggestions for Application

The competency model method is well suited for assessing individual learning needs. It may also be adapted for organizations or parts of them when desirable competencies are common to all involved.

There is an interesting spin-off application for the competency model itself. In organizational settings, it can be used verbatim as the basis for a performance evaluation system. This coupling of staff development and staff evaluation strengthens both.

Advantages to Competency Model Method

- Leads to an organized sequence of learnings

- Provides a complete set of learnings necessary for a particular job or role
- Provides a standard of behavior for any particular job or role
- Provides a convenient basis for designing orientation or basic training (new employees have not yet encountered problems)
- Is more adaptable (than problem analysis) to individual needs and individual pacing

Disadvantages to Competency Model Method

- Requires the relative continuity of both participants and educator
- Does not lead to immediate problem solution
- Requires a great deal of background information about behaviors required in meeting the model

Competency Model Worksheet

The following worksheet is provided for your use in conducting a competency model needs assessment. It is designed to be completed by participants if a democratic approach to needs assessment is used. When participants have individually completed the worksheet, you may use a separate worksheet to record the group averages and construct a group profile. The worksheet containing group data then becomes the first sheet in the *Workshop Staff Packet*. The *Group* item is for describing the participant group.

In order to make clearer the use of this worksheet, I will describe the options for use in each step of the competency model needs assessment.

61

1. *Developing a Competency Model* (refer to Step One in text)

   Once the competencies required for the particular role (or task) have been specified, they are entered in the column designated *Desired Competencies*. This may be done by you or by participants working from a master list. The space designated *Competency Model for* is used to describe the role or task for which the model is constructed.

2. *Discovering Present Levels of Performance* (refer to Step Two in text)

   When you are assessing participant competencies without consulting participants, you may complete the worksheet for individuals or the group as a whole based on whatever data you are using. When participants are asked to self-assess, they are provided with individual copies of the worksheet. A space is provided at the top left for their names. If the democratic approach is used, first have each participant complete the worksheet independently. You may then share with him other relevant data, such as supervisory assessments. Participants are then allowed the opportunity to revise their self-assessments if they desire. The notes at the bottom of the worksheet are provided as directions for participants in self-assessing.

   The assessment scale presented here differs from those commonly used in rating performance. Despite the negative implication, I believe this ($-$, $+$) rating scale to be more honest and adult than a sequence of positive numbers. It also aids in discrimination by forcing a choice between adequate and inadequate performance levels. In the directions, participants are asked to construct a profile by connecting the circled numbers with solid lines. At the completion of learning activities, they may self-assess again, connecting the new circled numbers with dotted lines. Comparison between the solid profile and the dotted one graphically reflects progress. In cases where continued growth is both desirable and possible, you may want to extend the scale to $(-5, +5)$ or even $(-9, +9)$.

3. *Specifying Needs*
The prospective adult learner is usually far better than anyone else at pinpointing exactly what he needs to learn in order to raise his performance to expected levels. Whatever approach you choose, the *Needs Learning* column is provided for recording this data.

4. *Separating Learning from Nonlearning Needs*
Again, the emphasis here is not on problem analysis. However, it may be clear that once a particular learning need has been met, other kinds of change or support will be required if the new behavior is to be used in real life. The *Nonlearning* need column is provided to record such data.

5. *Assigning Priorities*
The column indicated by "*#*" is reserved for the priority ranking. In arriving at group rankings, a simple average of individual rankings may produce unsatisfactory results if the average cancels out extreme needs. You might choose instead to arrive at a group ranking by giving a "1" to the competency receiving the largest number of individual "1" rankings, a "2" to the competency receiving the second largest number of "1" rankings, and so on. Another alternative is to have participants use their individual rankings as a basis for making decisions by concensus.

Only learning needs receive a priority ranking; related nonlearning needs take the same ranking.

6. *Testing Commitment*
   The worksheet containing group averages and the group profile is used in checking with both management and participants for commitment.

   In addition to the worksheet itself, I have provided a sample of a partially completed worksheet based on the example found in the text.

NEEDS ASSESSMENT: COMPETENCY MODEL

Name:	Group:

Competency Model for:

Desired (required) Competencies	Performance Assessment Scale		Needs		
	Inadequate	Adequate	Learning	#	Nonlearning
1.	(—) 3 2 1	(+) 1 2 3			
2.	3 2 1	1 2 3			
3.	3 2 1	1 2 3			
4.	3 2 1	1 2 3			
5.	3 2 1	1 2 3			
6.	3 2 1	1 2 3			
7.	3 2 1	1 2 3			
8.	3 2 1	1 2 3			
9.	3 2 1	1 2 3			
10.	3 2 1 (—)	1 2 3 (+)			

Directions: For each competency listed, circle the number that most accurately reflects your present level of performance. This is not an evaluation, but a tool to assist you in specifying your learning needs, so please be as honest as possible. Connect the circled numbers with solid lines. The pattern of these lines helps you see your strong and weak areas. For each negative number circled, describe in your own words what you think you need to learn to reach an adequate level of performance in that competency. If adequate performance, in your opinion, requires something in addition to what you will be learning, indicate this in the Nonlearning needs column. The column designated by (#) is for ranking your needs in priority order. Place a "1" by the need that is most important to you, a "2" by the next most important, etc.

65

NEEDS ASSESSMENT: COMPETENCY MODEL

Name: Tim Meek	Group: Line Supervisors, Operations

Competency Model for:
Line Supervision (Leadership)

Desired (required) Competencies	Performance Assessment Scale		Needs		
	Inadequate	Adequate	Learning	#	Nonlearning
1 A good line supervisor knows the three basic leadership styles; authoritarian, democratic, and laissez faire.	(—) 3 2 1	(+) 1 2 ③		3.	
2. A good line supervisor is competent in using all three styles.	3 ② 1	1 2 3	Need to use the authoritarian style effectively. (assertive behavior)	1.	Boss needs to close door.
3 A good line supervisor knows which style is appropriate to the specific employee and the specific situation.	3 2 1	1 ② 3		2.	
4.	3 2 1	1 2 3			
5.	3 2 1	1 2 3			
6.	3 2 1	1 2 3			
7.	3 2 1	1 2 3			
8.	3 2 1	1 2 3			
9.	3 2 1	1 2 3			
10.	3 2 1 (—)	1 2 3 (+)			

Directions: For each competency listed, circle the number that most accurately reflects your present level of performance. This is not an evaluation, but a tool to assist you in specifying your learning needs, so please be as honest as possible. Connect the circled numbers with solid lines. The pattern of these lines helps you see your strong and weak areas. For each negative number circled, describe in your own words what you think you need to learn to reach an adequate level of performance in that competency. If adequate performance, in your opinion, requires something in addition to what you will be learning, indicate this in the Nonlearning needs column. The column designated by (#) is for ranking your needs in priority order. Place a "1" by the need that is most important to you, a "2" by the next most important, etc.

NEEDS ASSESSMENT SIMPLIFIED

If the following analysis seems too harsh, remember that any discipline worthy of the name requires a little courage. The simplified needs assessment is for use only under the following limiting circumstances:

1. Some authority says "teach 'em that whether they want it or not."

2. Some participants say they want something whether they can use it or not.

3. A change of elements in the environment (guidelines, policies, procedures, laws) necessitates a briefing, whether anyone agrees or not.

4. "I don't care what they *think* they need, I *know* what they need."

If, under these circumstances, you still *choose* to go on with the workshop, or if you feel forced to, the needs assessment may be done as follows.

Problem Analysis Method Simplified

1. *Stating the problem*—simply repeat the limiting circumstance.

2. *Refining the problem statement*— no refinement needed. It is already in the form of a solution.

3. *Supporting the problem statement*—unless participants see a problem as a problem, it's not a problem. Don't try to support it.

4. *Finding the needs*—there is only one; the need for the educator to respond to the problem. You could, for the entertainment of participants, describe the values of the learning, but it is probably better to say it straight.

5. *Separate Learning from Nonlearning Needs*—under these circumstances, there's no difference.

6. *Assigning Priorities*—it *is* the priority.

7. *Testing Commitment*—you must be kidding.

Competency Model Method Simplified

1. *Developing a Competency Model*—simply state the behavior expected of participants at the end of the workshop. If no behavior is expected, say so.

2. *Discovering Present Level of Performance*—it is assumed to be inadequate.

68

3. *Specifying Needs—*whose? Yours or theirs? Repeat Step 1, describe the limiting circumstance, or hum *America.*

4. *Separating Learning from Non-learning Needs—*needs are needs are needs.

5. *Assigning Priorities—*redundant.

6. *Testing Commitment—*have participants pledge allegiance.

STYLE VARIATIONS
(Applies to both methods)

Authoritarian Approach

In the extreme case, the educator talks to himself (or other educators). If he is a moderate authoritarian he may include supervisors and/or top brass in the deliberations. Whether legitimately or not, this is usually justified on the grounds that participants are unavailable, too far away, unknown, or lacking in sufficient expertise to participate.

Laissez Faire Approach

In the extreme case, the educator sits silently while participants (each and all, if possible) tell him what they want. Management's views are not solicited. Whether merited or not, this procedure is usually justified on the grounds that the educator should not interfere with adult self-direction. If he is a moderate laissez faire educator he becomes active, adding his own ideas and guiding the process.

Democratic Approach

If he is in the middle, the educator talks with everyone he can get his hands on: top brass, supervisors, and participants. The wise democratic educator begins at the top from whence all blessings flow. He then gets the views of immediate supervisors, and finally those of participants. He also talks a lot himself. The process tends to be more democratic if the assessment at each level is completed independently and then negotiated for agreement (in organizations some men really *are* more equal than others). In toto, the democratic approach to needs assessment is justified on the grounds that all those affected should have a say.

My View on the Matter

The extreme laissez faire approach may occasionally be appropriate with very independent adults. Often, however, it results in frustration and wasted time. The moderate laissez faire approach is essentially democratic when no organization is involved. When an organization is involved, this approach will not often serve the organization's needs.

On the other hand, the extreme authoritarian approach creates needs in a vacuum, and consequently seldom serves anyone's purpose. The moderate authoritarian approach may sometimes be appropriate when there are restraints on time or money, but it gives rise to the added need to motivate the participant or to reinforce him like mad.

In my opinion, the democratic approach is the best for most worlds. When this approach is used successfully it serves everyone's needs. Motivation is high and the learning climate good. When organizations are involved the democratic approach eliminates the need to modify the work environment for reinforcement of the new behaviors. It begins with mutual agreement, with a contract binding both participants and management to using and reinforcing the new learned behaviors.

Participants and management, not the educator, are in the best position to understand and arrange the variables of the environment to acccommodate new behaviors. Therefore, it is the simplest, cheapest, and surest way to get results. The educator's responsibility ends at the door of the workshop. If the new behaviors are learned, he has done his job.

There is one problem with the democratic approach. If you use it in working with an extremely authoritarian organization, it acts much like a time bomb.

ALTERNATIVES

Since needs assessment is an inescapably complex task, you may want to consider certain alternatives for modifying the methods (as described here) when group size, available time, or distance from the participants becomes a problem. Following are a few ideas.

A large number of prospective participants presents a problem for both methods of needs assessment. It might be possible to break the participants into several smaller groups for needs assessment purposes or to break the proposed workshop into several smaller workshops. If neither is possible, a representative advisory group can yield satisfactory results provided that 1) the group is truly representative and 2) that the remainder of the participants recognize it as such.

Obviously the methods presented here can be time consuming. When the educator has a continuing relationship with the organization or the individual participants, a full scale needs assessment need not be conducted more than once a year. Periodic short sessions can be scheduled throughout the year for review and revision of the needs assessment data.

If the educator will work with the group for only one workshop, and if the time available for needs assessment is limited, it is necessary to define the scope of the needs assessment by:

1) Limiting the number of problems to be dealt with in the problem analysis method, or

2) Limiting the number of competencies to be considered for the competency model.

The alternative of cutting out steps in the procedure should not be considered.

Normally, distance in miles between the educator and participants becomes a problem only for a consultant. Given this circumstance, the consultant educator has three options:

1. If he uses the competency model method, he may have the worksheets completed by mail and review the results with the participants at the workshop itself. In this case, he should be prepared to make some modifications on the spot.

   The problem analysis method is not amenable to mail because of the complexity of problem analysis.

2. The consultant educator may invite participants to a workshop centered around a particular topic or concern. Their attendance should indicate that they have some needs in the general direction of the topic. Even so, a more detailed assessment should be conducted at the beginning of the workshop

3. The consultant educator may design a workshop based on a needs assessment conducted by someone on location, provided it is thorough.

Again it is wise to check the assessment with participants at the beginning of the workshop and to be
prepared to make modifications.

SPECIFYING LEARNING OBJECTIVES

When talking about plans, people tend to use a variety of words that say roughly the same thing. One such family of words includes *goal, purpose, objective, end,* and *intent.* There have been a number of attempts to standardize the use of these words, including some rigorous definitions that arrange them in a pyramid according to the degree of importance. For this book I have chosen the word *objective* and it is used in the military sense:

"Our objective is to take hill 25397!"

In educational circles a number of words compete to precede objective. As a result, we hear such combinations as *behavioral* objective, *educational* objective, *terminal* objective, *performance* objective, *instructional* objective, *teaching* objective, and *learning* objective. In fairness it could be said that these modifiers tend to describe the various learning theories more than they describe the objectives to which they are attached. In this book I settled on the word *learning* for at least three reasons:

1. It describes what the participant will do, not my efforts in helping him do it.

2. An adult can make a commitment to the objective as his, rather than merely mine.

3. It is a common, everyday kind of word.

Now that we have settled that dust somewhat, why the word *specifying*? I do not use *setting, determining,* or even *developing,* since those words imply arbitrary decisions unrelated to the needs assessment. The need sets the objective! What you are doing *here* is attempting to make the objective extremely *clear.* The reason you are doing it is to make clear to yourself and to others where you are going. This enables the group to stay together during the learning experience and to know when the objective has been reached. Can you imagine the result if a sergeant said to his platoon leaders, "Our objective is to take some hill or other!"

STYLE VARIATIONS

A look at the style variations in specifying learning objectives reveals a curious phenomenon. On both the authoritarian and laissez faire extremes, there is a tendency to do nothing observable with objectives. They neither state, nor write, nor pay attention to objectives. For the really hard-line authoritarian the attitude seems to be "that's my business," or "they'll learn what I teach them," or "I know what I mean." For the laissez faire hard-liner it appears to be something like "whatever comes out is the objective," or "all objectives are worthwhile."

If forced to state objectives, extreme authoritarians will usually describe their planned activities ("imparting knowledge of—," "instilling the value of—," or "demonstrating the use of—") or list a series of topics ("classroom techniques," "management styles," "communication"). And under compulsion, extreme laissez faire practitioners tend to say such things as "developing awareness of—," "exploring the uses of—," or "discovering hidden potentials within—."

Still on the laissez faire side, but in the moderate position, there is considerable reliance on objectives. Their main purpose, however, is to serve as points of departure from which general directions can be taken in the continuing quest for learning. Individual side trips and sojourns are valued. The end is a beginning, and getting there is a matter of individual judgement. To this group, learning is a *multilayering* process with a great many of the layers out of sight. Accordingly, objectives that attempt to describe a learning outcome with great specificity are at best foolish since many of the important learnings are not observable. For this group of educators, the phrase *terminal objective* is fightin' words, denying the complex, various, and continuous nature of learning.

Back on the authoritarian side, but many miles from the despotic extreme, is an approach to objectives exactly opposite the one just described. For moderate authoritarians, objectives (behavioral, terminal, etc.) are a must. Furthermore, to be useful an objective should describe precisely the expected learning outcome. In fact, they would say that if you can't see it, it doesn't exist; or if it does exist, it is insignificant and unworthy of serious attention. This group falls on the determinist side of the theory fence, while the moderate laissez faire group are freewillers.

Before going on, I think I should again caution that the terms authoritarian, laissez faire, and democratic used throughout this book are no more than broad brush-stroke descriptions of somewhat consistent educational styles or approaches. As such, these styles should be seen as a reflection of the educator's orientation toward the individual human organism in the learning endeavor. They reflect the educator's understanding of how learning occurs, the influence of which can be seen in the various procedures of his educational practice. As such, the styles are neither good nor bad. Like the planets in orbit around the sun, each style is nearer to or farther from the truth depending on where it is found in relation to a particular aspect of educational practice.

Where, then, is the democratic group in the particular aspect called specifying objectives? We find the democrats using objectives like banners, as a means of keeping everyone together in the process of meeting mutually agreeable needs. Further, they seem to feel that it is easier to keep everyone together when all have approximately the same understanding of the objective. Like the serious authoritarians, but for different reasons, they attempt to make their objectives as precise as possible.

MY OPINION IN THIS MATTER

I am torn on this one. No matter how carefully I write objectives, no matter how many objectives I write for a particular learning experience, and no matter who participates in writing them, there is always a good deal of valuable learning that occurs which is not captured by the objectives. In contributing their experience, adults tend to carry the learning above and beyond the call of objectives. In groups, objectives that carefully specify the expected outcome tend to ignore individual differences.

On the other hand, the failure to carefully specify objectives means that nobody can really tell if anything was accomplished. Such an ambiguous outcome is not in the best interests of organizations. It can even be argued that the individual, too, is often ill-served by overly general objectives. If he is serious about achieving a particular competency, if it is crucial to his well-being, he will want to know exactly what it is and if he has achieved it. How often in learning situations has each of us experienced the feeling of understanding, only to have the feeling break down in confusion in the real world? Further, common sense tells us that global objectives tend to overwhelm us and that we are much more likely to get started if we can clearly see the next simple step.

A possible way out of the dilemma is to see specific learning objectives as the *minimum* competency desired or required. If there is no minimum, if it truly is a matter of individual choice or preference, then a simple statement of possibility seems to be enough. In working with organizations, however, I have found that there is almost always a minimum (whether explicit or not) and that it is consistent with the organization's purposes.

Specific learning objectives that clearly describe the expected outcomes serve two additional purposes:

1. They become road maps in designing learning activities and in selecting resources for learning.

2. They tend to dispel unrealistic and negative expectations. Everyone feels better when they expect to accomplish needed and agreed upon

competencies. Consequently, specific learning objectives are used before the workshop as a basis for goal agreement with management and at the beginning of the workshop for goal agreement between the educator and participants.

***   ***   ***

The remainder of this chapter describes fully the characteristics and structure of specific learning objectives. Related to this is a description of how general learning objectives can be used to organize the specific ones. There are sample worksheets that may help you in writing both, and an opportunity for you to "try your hand at it," after reading "The Sad Story of Farmer Brown."

WRITING GENERAL AND SPECIFIC LEARNING OBJECTIVES

General Learning Objectives

A general learning objective (GLO) describes in general and positive terms what the participant (learner) is expected to be able to do as a result of the learning activities. For example, "After struggling with this chapter, the reader will demonstrate his competency in specifying objectives."

As presented here, the main utility of general learning objectives is in organizing a disconnected string of specific objectives. Problem analysis yields a random assortment of learning needs; to a lesser degree competency models also yield a random assortment. The general learning objective serves as a kind of umbrella under which related learning needs can be grouped. Needs may be related by a procedure (such as specifying objectives), by a discrete body of knowledge (such as learning theory), by observable patterns (such as group dynamics), by functions of a job (such as scheduling), by particular role requirements (such as disciplining a child), and so forth. In the scheme of things GLO's are not as broad as the purposes of this book or the objectives of a course. Seldom are they as narrow as a specific learning objective. When relatively few specific learning objectives are involved, the general one may be omitted with no damage to the plan.

Types of Learning

As a means of breaking learning into more manageable pieces, let's take a quick look at yet another contested area in learning theory. Many theorists feel that learning cannot be described by a single process. They believe that there are several types (domains, areas) of learning, each characterized by its own separate and distinct process and each requiring its own learning or teaching strategy. As usual there is no general agreement on what the types are, how many there are, or a system for classifying them. Among types suggested are motor skills, intellectual skills, cognitive strategies, attitudes, values, interests, affective skills, and reflective thinking.

I have settled on three types labeling them with commonly understood words:

1. Knowledge learning
2. Skill learning
3. Attitude learning

83

I do not suggest that these three types are a correct and complete description of reality, but that they encompass all the learning I have seen and break it into useful categories without wandering off into endless distinctions. I do not claim that these are the best words to describe the three types, but that most people understand essentially what I mean by them. In order that you might know **exactly** what I mean, let's take the three types one at a time, see what they include, and look at some other words that could have been used to describe them.

1. **Knowledge learning** includes the recognition, comparison, correlation, integration, perhaps creation, and storage of all kinds of data or information. Other words that could have been used include *cognitive, intellectual,* and *understanding.*

2. **Skill learning** involves the notion of repetition, practice, or habit. As such it includes all procedures, operations, activities, methods, and techniques involving repetition. Occasionally there seems to be an overlap of knowledge learning and skill learning, such as when knowledge is used to solve a problem. But applying knowledge to the solution of a single problem does not necessarily demonstrate a skill. Solving a single problem may demonstrate no more than a fortuitous combination of data—

"You accidentally got it right."
Skill at problem solving is demonstrated by **repeated** success in solving a variety of problems requiring a variety of knowledge. Skill is the method or technique, while knowledge is the data supporting it.

Another term sometimes used to describe this type of learning is *psychomotor*.

3. **Attitude learning** includes the formation of values, emotional responses (feelings), and tendencies (interests, preferences, tastes, likes, and dislikes). Here the word *attitude* is used as in "What is your attitude about this matter?"

   Other words that could have been used are *affective* and *emotional*.

These three classifications provide one way to analyze learning needs.

The importance of this scheme in analyzing learning needs can be illustrated rather simply. The inadequacy (or lack) of a certain behavior may be explained in four ways:

1. The individual has incorrect or inadequate knowledge.

2. The individual lacks the skill to use the knowledge he has.

3. The individual doesn't want to use his knowledge and skill.

4. Any combination of the above.

A general learning objective, then, may also be seen as a means of grouping the different types of learning required to produce a particular behavior or set of behaviors.

Specific Learning Objectives

A specific learning objective (SLO) describes as precisely as possible what the learner will be able to do as a result of a learning activity or series of learning activities which focus directly on a particular previously identified need.

In writing SLO's the point is to make them as explicit as possible. They should include the following four ingredients:

1. A specification of the **type of learning** at which the SLO aims: knowledge, skill, or attitude. Each SLO should address only one type of learning.

2. A description of the **observable behavior** that will demonstrate that the learning occurred. Observable behaviors are those you can see, hear, smell, etc.

3. A statement of an acceptable (minimum) **level of performance** for the

learned behavior. Such levels (standards) describe how much, how well, how quickly, etc. These levels should not be arbitrary; they should approximate the requirements of the real life situation. Since many real life behaviors cannot be measured with clocks, scales, and yardsticks, the judge(s) should be specified i.e., the participant himself, the instructor, the boss, a special consultant, peer group, or any combination of these.

4. A description of the **conditions** under which the performance will be measured. Conditions include both permissions and restrictions. They specify what the learner may and may not use to assist him in performing. The conditions should again approximate or simulate the real life situation.

Perhaps it would be helpful to look at the last three ingredients in light of the type of learning involved. The chart on the next page is designed for this purpose.

LEARNING TYPES/TYPICAL SPECIFICATIONS

	KNOWLEDGE LEARNING	SKILL LEARNING	ATTITUDE LEARNING
1. OBSERVABLE BEHAVIORS	List, describe, state, report, discuss, debate, critique, etc.	Demonstrate, role play, lead, perform, solve, assemble. . . .	Role play, discuss, touch, hold, smile, laugh, cry, approach, avoid. . . .
2. PERFORMANCE LEVELS	**Standards** Seven out of ten, the major points, the importance of the five theories. . . . **Judges** To your own satisfaction, in the opinion of authorities, to my (instructor's) satisfaction, as judged by bosses, peers. . . .	**Standards** Once, twice . . .; seven out of ten, all the parts, the six steps, with no more than three errors, in ten minutes. . . . **Judges** To the satisfaction of peers, bosses, instructors, experts, yourself. . . .	**Standards** Convincingly, comfortably, unflinchingly, unhesitantly. . . . **Judges** To your own satisfaction; in the opinion of leaders, bosses, peers, etc.; as felt by whoever. . . .
3. CONDITIONS	**Permissions** Given the article on, with aid of notes and materials. . . . **Restrictions** Without aid of notes, without coaching, without the sample/model. . . .	**Permissions** Given the formulas, given the parts, given the situation, with aid of notes and materials. . . . **Restrictions** Without aid of notes, without coaching, without the sample/model. . . .	**Permissions** In any way that seems natural, when you feel like it, if you feel free to. . . . **Restrictions** Without talking, hitting, using your hands, moving away. . . .

Things get a little touchy when you deal with attitudes. Since they are inside people, they can only be observed indirectly. Only the person himself knows the reality of his attitudes, and he can convincingly "fake it" if the rewards or penalties are great enough.

When attitude problems clearly exist, it is most productive to let employees and their bosses deal with them by working out rewards or penalties on the job, allowing you to limit your practice to knowledge and skills. But if it is your responsibility to plan a workshop to cover attitude problems, the following precautions should be taken:

1. Allow participants to be their own judges.

2. Make participation strictly voluntary.

3. Bind yourself and participants to strict ground rules.

You cannot change attitudes by preaching. New information or new skills often bring about the needed attitude change. For more difficult cases, a sensitizing experience may get results, but it may also lead to harm. Think long and hard before planning such an experience and be sure that a competent person is to be in charge.

If you are interested in catching the general drift of attitudes related to the learning, there are a couple of simple and nonthreatening procedures to follow:

1. Openly explore the implications of attitudes for the required new behavior, but leave the formation of them up to the individual (which means having **no** attitude objective!). Without directly asking, listen for spontaneous comments like:

- "That really hit me!"
- "I never knew he (they) felt like that."
- "I could never do that!"

Keep the results to yourself.

2. In his book *Developing Attitude Toward Learning*, Mager defines attitude as follows:

> "Actually, 'attitude' is a word used to
> refer to a *general tendency* of an indi-
> vidual to act in a certain way under
> certain conditions."³

He goes on to explain that our *perception* of a person's attitude is based on his observable behavior. Consequently we can simply note a participant's avidness in approaching or avoiding the learning in question. Again, you should exercise great care in use of the data.

Some Examples

Are you confused? That's the normal reaction at this point. Let's put it all together and see if that clears the air.

Going back to the example of a GLO stated earlier in this chapter, I will specify the remainder of my intent for this chapter. I hope that it is yours, also.

GLO: After struggling with this chapter, the reader will demonstrate his competency in specifying objectives.

SLO #1: After reading the discussion of GLO's found in this chapter, the reader will demonstrate his **knowledge** describing the function of GLO's to the first person he can find. He will do this to his own satisfaction and in his own words without referring to mine.

SLO #2: After exploring the discussion concerning types of learning, the reader will demonstrate his **knowledge** by naming aloud at least three learning types and arguing for the inclusion of any others if he cares to. This will be done to his own satisfaction with reference to the book only after he has named the three.

After pondering the section entitled *Specific Learning Objectives* (SLO's), the reader will demonstrate:

SLO #3: His **knowledge** of SLO ingredients by stating and describing three out of four ingredients to his own satisfaction (his child, if available, might coach him) and without referring to the book.

SLO #4: His **knowledge** of SLO ingredients by picking out all four ingredients in SLO #5. He may glance back over the preceding pages if useful.

SLO #5: After reading "The Sad Story of Farmer Brown" (p. 95), the reader will demonstrate his **skill** in specifying objectives by writing one GLO and three SLO's about this story. In doing this,

91

he may refer to anything in the book, and he may use one of the sample worksheets if desired. After checking his objectives against those listed at the end of the story, he may judge his own competency.

SLO #6: After struggling with the entire chapter, the reader will demonstrate his **attitude** toward it by what he does next.

You will notice that the first phrase of each SLO above begins with a description of the learning activity. This convention is optional. If you choose to write your SLO's in this manner, you may not be ready to specify learning activities until you have completed the design (see Chapter Four). When I initially write the objective, this phrase is commonly either blank or general, i.e., "at the completion of the learning activity. . . ." You will notice that the type of learning is set in bold type. On a handwritten or typed page, underlining the type of learning provides quick cross reference with the detailed design of learning activities.

The style in writing objectives is not important; the specificity of them is. Most of the time I use complete sentences. As you can see from the above examples, the format and arrangement may vary considerably. On the following page you will find a sample worksheet that does not require complete sentences. Following that is a worksheet that does. On both worksheets "Learning Needs" refers to needs recorded on Worksheet #1 for which the particular SLO has been specified. Choose a style comfortable to you.

GENERAL AND SPECIFIC LEARNING OBJECTIVES

Problem or Desired Competency:	Group:

General Learning Objective:

Specific Learning Objectives

SLO #1:	Type of Learning:	Learning Needs:
Observable Behavior:		
Performance Standard:		
Conditions:		

SLO #2:	Type of Learning:	Learning Needs:
Observable Behavior:		
Performance Standard:		
Conditions:		

SLO # 3:	Type of Learning:	Learning Needs:
Observable Behavior:		
Performance Standard:		
Conditions:		

SLO #4:	Type of Learning:	Learning Needs:
Observable Behavior:		
Performance Standard:		
Conditions:		

SLO #5:	Type of Learning:	Learning Needs:
Observable Behavior:		
Performance Standard:		
Conditions:		

SLO #6:	Type of Learning:	Learning Needs:
Observable Behavior:		
Performance Standard:		
Conditions:		

SLO #7:	Type of Learning:	Learning Needs:
Observable Behavior:		
Performance Standard:		
Conditions:		

SLO #8:	Type of Learning:	Learning Needs:
Observable Behavior:		
Performance Standard:		
Conditions:		

GENERAL AND SPECIFIC LEARNING OBJECTIVES

Problem or Desired Competency:	Group:

Learning Needs:

General Learning Objective (GLO):

Specific Learning Objectives (SLO):
SLO #1:

SLO #2:

SLO #3:

SLO #4:

SLO #5:

SLO #6:

SLO #7:

SLO #8:

THE SAD STORY OF FARMER BROWN

One day while strolling down a pleasant country lane minding my own whistling, I came upon Farmer Brown standing by his mailbox crying. Now I had known Farmer Brown for years, and I knew him to be a good natured, happy man. Somewhat alarmed at the sight of his tears, I said, "Goodness, whatever is the matter?"

He shook his head sadly, looking at a stack of bills in his hand. "Ah reckon ah'm goin' broke," he said.

"My, that is something to cry about, inflation being what it is and all. . . ."

"Naw, it ain't the inflation. It's the dad blamed fuel shortage," he broke in.

Seeing that he was not going to offer an explanation, I queried, "Not enough gas for the tractor?"

"Don't need no tractor. Already got in the crops," he said, frowning slightly at my city-boy ignorance.

"Well, what is the problem?" I asked, undaunted.

"They rationed mah 'lectricity, and ah ain't got no gas to run the generator for mah milkin' machine," he said.

I thought I could vaguely hear cows bellowing in the distance. "Why don't you milk them by hand?" I said.

"Been tryin' to," he said, "but me 'n my wife just cain't keep up. There's thirty-eight cows over there. Reckon I'll have to shoot some of 'em. Sell "em for soap."

"That seems a waste," I sympathized. "Can't you hire some men to help you?"

"Ain't got no money to pay no hands," he said. "Got it all tied up in that dad burned milkin' machine, and the bank owns most of that. And hollerin' for more." He looked at the bills.

Afraid he would start crying again, I said, "But don't you have a couple of grown boys?"

"Yup. Seth's nigh on to eighteen, and Bob is pushin' seventeen. But them boys couldn't find the hind end of a cow. Spend all their time at that new-fangled school. Or chasin' skirts."

"Well, they could learn, couldn't they?" I said.

"Ain't got the patience to teach 'em," he said, "even if they was willin'. Besides, them cows gotta be milked seven days a week, and them boys is just downright lazy."

"Maybe I could help," I offered. "My work involves helping people learn things."

"What d'ya know 'bout cows?" he asked, "or boys neither, for that matter."

"I know quite a bit about boys," I said, "and enough about cows."

"I don't know," he said, "I'd have to see it. Besides, mah ol' milk pails are darn near rusted out."

"Clearly you'll have to get new milk pails," I said, "but in the meantime let's see what we can find out about the rest of this problem."

In talking it over some more we established the following facts:

1. Farmer Brown and his wife had roughly the same competency in milking, that is, each could take all of a cow's milk in about 15 minutes. (This is a bit slow, but both had arthritis.)

2. If they staked the cows in a row they could go from one cow to another without losing any time in between.

96

3. Given his other chores, Farmer Brown could only spare 3 hours a day on milking; his wife, only 2 hours. That meant:

15 min./cow=4 cows/mnhr. x 5 mnhr.=20 cows

leaving 18 cows for Seth and Bob.

4. What with homework and girls, Seth and Bob could spare 3 hours a day. That meant:

18 cows ÷ 6 man-hours=3 cows/boy/hour.

5. Even if we could get the boys up to that level, there was still a tough motivation problem in the seven-days-a-week nature of the work.

On the following page, you will find my proposed learning objectives. Before you look at them, you might want to try your hand at it. Everything you need is in the story.

GLO: At the completion of the training program, Seth and Bob will be competent in cow milking.

SLO #1: After studying the charts on cow anatomy and physiology, as well as observing firsthand, Seth and Bob will each demonstrate his **knowledge** of cow anatomy by pointing to the hind end, the bag, the teats, the tail, and the back hooves and calling them by their "country" names. Each will do this to Farmer Brown's satisfaction without the aid of charts or coaching from his brother.

SLO #2: After demonstration and practice of proper milking procedures, each boy will demonstrate his milking **skill** by milking at least three different cows in a one-hour period, spilling no more than a cup of milk (Farmer Brown was feeling lenient). He will do this without the aid of rubber gloves and to the satisfaction of Farmer Brown and the cows.

> ASIDE: Farmer Brown was convinced of the advantages of profit sharing. As a result (and much to my relief) the SLO dealing with attitude was discarded. He was convinced when he saw the proposed SLO for attitudes, below:

SLO #3: At the completion of a sensitizing experience on the joys of of milking, each boy will demonstrate a positive **attitude** toward cow milking by spontaneously saying something like: "Wow, I really love milking!" or "Where have these cows been all my life!" or I'd rather milk than eat!" He will do this without glancing at the *Playboy* pinups hanging on the walls.

Unfortunately the Farmer Brown Story has a sad ending. There was also a shortage of milk pails.

***   ***   ***

If your learning objectives are still a little vague at this point, don't worry about it. It took me months to get it down. They get better with practice. Go find yourself another story and write some more.

98

SELECTING RESOURCES

Resources for learning are found in two realms, the animate and the inanimate. In the animate realm, you are interested in such organisms as educators, assistants, group leaders, consultants, authorities (including bosses), and the participants themselves. In addition to these individual resources, you must also consider their possible combinations and interactions.

From the inanimate realm you are interested in such objects as books, articles, films, tapes, case studies, games, and simulations. In addition to selecting from among these resources, you must also consider the effects of the environment in which they will be combined and utilized.

In selecting resources for learning you are primarily concerned with three things:

1. Are they the best available for achieving the learning objectives?

2. Are they consistent with the style of your educational practice?

3. Are they consistent with the educational style that the participants (and their organizations) expect?

Your decisions will reflect a blending of these three concerns.

BEST FOR ACHIEVING OBJECTIVE

The most common mistake made in planning workshops occurs at this point. Too often workshops are built around the latest/hottest book, article, or expert; participant needs take a back seat. Objectives (if stated) are merely rationalizations for showing off the resource. Worse still is the practice of involving participants in needs assessment and then subjecting them to stimulating irrelevancies. If needs and objectives are taken seriously, the intention is to select learning resources that lead to the objectives.

EDUCATOR'S STYLE

If the style is authoritarian, the selected resources will usually dominate the learning, leaving little room for participant expertise or opinion. If laissez faire, participants will usually be seen as the primary resource for learning and will be involved in selecting any other resources. If democratic, learning resources will be selected that provide a foundation or framework for participants to build upon. Whatever the predominant style, the selected resources should be consistent with it.

PARTICIPANT STYLE EXPECTATIONS

Participants (and the organizations they represent) expect to find certain educational styles in the workshops they attend. If they expect a very authoritarian (authoritative) style, then loose or open-to-question resources will disturb them. If they expect a laissez faire

100

style, then the Bible itself will be rejected. In addition to considering your own style, it would be useless to select resources that embody an educational style repugnant to participants.

ELEMENTS TO CONSIDER

In both the literature and practice of adult education, the thing that perhaps causes the most confusion is the tremendous assortment of items to be considered in planning and conducting learning activities. As a means of clearing the fog, I have devised a list of twelve standard elements that encompasses most of these items. In this chapter and many of the following ones, this list is used as the basis for describing and analyzing the various tasks that produce successful workshops. The twelve elements are:

1. Materials
2. Staff
3. Consultants
4. Participants
5. Structure
6. Aids
7. Facilities
8. Accommodations
9. Food and Refreshments
10. Dates
11. Travel
12. Promotion

In most cases the numerical sequence of the above elements corresponds with the order in which they might best be considered. In Chapter 4 I modify the order but retain the numerical designations due to their usefulness on the worksheets. Not all the elements are applicable to every activity, and this is noted in the text. Additionally, it was necessary for the sake of completeness to add elements at certain points; they are numbered thirteen, fourteen, etc. In this chapter, I have added a thirteenth element.

Let's consider the elements one by one and see how they apply to selecting resources for learning.

1. Materials

By materials I mean those inanimate resources that often form the foundations for learning. Such resources include the following:

   a) Printed material—books, articles, excerpts, case studies. . . .

   b) Audio-visual material—films, tapes, slides, videotapes, multimedia. . . .

   c) Packaged material — programmed instruction, games, simulations. . . .

Each type has its advantages and disadvantages. The important thing is to select learning materials that contribute to attaining the objective. If the needs assessment is well done, then the level of difficulty is already prescribed and contained in the objective. Materials that cover more ground than necessary should be edited.

2. Staff

Staff should be selected for their content expertise or their skill in facilitating the learning. We should make our intention clear for each person chosen. Potential staff includes the educator planning the workshop, assistants, supervisors, and other authorities from any organizations involved. These individuals should be selected on the basis of their potential contributions to the learning, rather than for politics or public relations. Their styles should form a consistent pattern; they must be able to work together.

3. Consultants

There are only three reasons for bringing in outsiders: 1) they are the best content people for the job, 2) they are essential as facilitators in the learning process, or 3) they are free from the stigma of a "prophet in his own land." Again, their roles, content ranges, and styles should be considered. If you decide to use consultants, you should immediately check their availability and interest. Consultants book themselves several months in advance.

4. Participants

If participants are to be considered a resource for their own learning, you should make a rough estimate of their possible contributions. In addition, you must consider just how their resources will be blended with those selected from the elements above.

5. Structure

Structure means the way in which the materials and people are put together to accomplish learning. Structural options include those for:

> a) *individuals*: they may be on chairs, behind tables, facing the speaker, back in their rooms. . . .
>
> b) *groups:* there may be pairs, triads, etc.; they may be arranged in cir-

103

cles, squares, lines; isolated or interacting. . . .

c) *staff:* they may be up front, within
groups, in back, out in the
lobby. . . .

d) *combinations of the above:* approaching infinity.

For a more complete listing see p. 153.

At this point we are concerned only with stating
some tentative conclusions regarding the value of certain structures as a resource for learning.

6. Aids

Aids are the various props that support the learning.
These include such things as:

a) content aids—charts, graphs, projectors. . . .

b) staff aids—blackboards, easels, newsprint, tape. . . .

c) participant aids—pencils, paper, instructions. . . .

Detailed decisions about aids can be made only in
the design stage. At this point, simply state your likes,
dislikes, and theories concerning the helpfulness of any,
all, or certain of these aids.

7. Facilities

At this point all that is required is a tentative judgement on the nature of the facilities needed for the workshop. Should the facilities be peaceful, plain, luxurious, etc? Should they be commuter facilities (in-house, in town) or dormitory facilities (in another city, in the country, etc.)? How large should they be, etc.?

8. Accommodations

These need be considered only if we conclude that participants should get away from it all for purposes of the workshop. If so then pleasantness, comfort, and amenities might merit some thought.

9. Food and Refreshments

What will coffee, tea, cokes, etc., contribute to learning effectiveness? Their importance varies with the time of day and the length of the workshop. If the workshop spans a customary mealtime (or several of them) decide whether group meals or individual arrangements will better suit the learning. Group meals get everyone back at the same time; individual arrangements allow time for "digesting" the learning.

10. Dates

Not relevant at this point.

11. Travel

Needs to be considered at this time only if it is, in itself, part of the learning.

12. Promotion

Dealt with in later chapters.

13. Time

You might consider whether a fast-paced or more leisurely workshop would be better for learning. Greater detail is a matter for the design stage.

***   ***   ***

On the next page you will find Worksheet 3 for recording your tentative resource selections. This worksheet (and several to follow) is organized around the list of standard elements. For the most part, the worksheet is either self-explanatory or explained by the text of this chapter. It does, however, include one feature that should be explained: cross-referencing by GLO and SLO. In the text I discussed the selection of resources generically; in practice it is often useful to pin certain of the resources down to specific objectives, and the vertical *SLO* column is for that purpose. For the elements that affect all SLO's equally, write *ALL* in the SLO column. Each GLO requires a separate worksheet.

In addition, you will find a format for permanent maintenance of a learning resource inventory. This format is designed so that resources may be grouped according to the content areas with which you commonly work. As an example, Group A might be General Management, Group B might be Supervisory Skills, etc.

LEARNING RESOURCES SELECTION

Workshop	Group

GLO:

Reference: The notes on this sheet represent initial thoughts regarding the best resources for achieving the above General Learning Objective Each SLO relating to this GLO is cross-referenced by number (see Worksheet Two)

RESOURCES

SLO #	

	1. Materials:
	Title Type Style
	  a)
	  b)
	  c)
	  d)

	2. Staff
	Name Role Style
	  a)
	  b)
	  c)
	  d)

	3. Consultants
	Name Role Style Available
	  a)
	  b)
	  c)
	  d)

	4. Participants (possible contributions to learning/by SLO)
	  a)
	  b)
	  c)
	  d)

	5. Structure (desirable/by SLO #)
	  a)
	  b)
	  c)
	  d)

	6. Aids (preferences by SLO#) Content Staff Participants
	7. Facilities (qualities desired)
	8. Accommodations (desirable qualities, if applicable)
	9. Food and Refreshments
N/A	10. Dates, 11. Travel, 12. Promotion—Not applicable.
	13. Time: (fast paced or slow paced, preferences by SLO #)

LEARNING RESOURCE INVENTORY

Group A   Group B   Group C

MATERIALS (grouped according to general content)

Group	Title	Source	Type	Style	Cost
A					
B					
C					

POTENTIAL STAFF (in-house, grouped according to specialty)

Group	Name	Department	Specialty	Style
A				
B				
C				

CONSULTANTS (group according to specialty)

Group	Name	Address	Specialty	Style	Fee
A					
B					
C					

AIDS (available)

Type	Location	Cost, if any

FACILITIES

Name	Location	Qualities	Cost

DESIGNING LEARNING ACTIVITIES 4

As the word implies, *designing* learning activities is an artistic endeavor. Some writers in the field add the word *still*, meaning that designing is not yet a science, but, by the Grace of God and their own diligence, it soon will be. It is never clear what kind of scientific behavior they have in mind. Is it developing formulas for designs? Is it posing hypotheses which then would be proven or discounted experimentally, with participants acting as guinea pigs? Or is it simply a more orderly way of arranging the elements? If the last, the apologetic *still* smacks of scientism or an ignorance of art. Every serious art form has an orderly way of arranging the elements; libraries are filled with critical books documenting it. Without apology, therefore, I call a good learning design a work of art and high art at that; and I invite you to join in the joy of creation.

The design of learning activities is similar to the structure of novels. Central to the novel is a plot: a sequence of events or episodes arranged so that they build to a climax. The workshop designer arranges a sequence of events so that they lead to objectives. In a novel the author early establishes a conflict which must be resolved through the plot. For workshops the moving force (motivation) is based on the need to resolve the dis-

109

parity (conflict) between present and desired behavior established at the very first by needs assessment.

Workshop sessions can be compared to chapters in a novel. Each session of a workshop begins by setting the tone (serious, light . . .) and a climate or mood (calm, open, threatening, oppressive . . .). It continues by previewing the events to come and moves through designed activities to the intended learning (the important information revealed in each chapter). The feedback at the end of each session lets the participant know how he has done, how each chapter ends.

To carry the analogy a bit further, the novel engages the reader in both intellectual and emotional experiences. The best adult workshops do the same. A good novel engages the reader in the action, and the same can be said for a good workshop.

Many more parallels could be mentioned; they are left for you to discover.

THE ELEMENTS

In the literature of adult education, writers have described the task of designing learning activities in terms that might be better suited to the stage magician. "Throw all the elements in a hat, turn around three times, and **PRESTO!** Out pops a design."

Above I described design as an artistic endeavor; one that leads to an orderly arrangement of elements. Below is a modified sequence of the twelve standard elements (and a few others) which suggests a practical, orderly way to move from sketchy ideas to a completed design. In order to provide a quick cross-reference to the various worksheets, I have retained the original numerical designations for the elements; they are found in parentheses following the element titles. As you

110

consider the various elements for your design, refer to Worksheet 3, Learning Resources Selection, on which you recorded tentative decisions about a number of them. Worksheet 4, found later in this chapter, provides a format for the actual written design. In the following description of the design process, comments such as "sketch in," "pencil them into," etc., refer to the use of this form.

Materials (1)

One of the best and easiest things to do in beginning a design is to thoroughly scrutinize any materials that you plan to use in the workshop. You may decide to throw them away. You may become absorbed in them as a way to avoid getting started. What you are really trying to do is figure out a way to help the participants "get into them" or a way to get them into the participants. Usually the materials have a pattern of development which may suggest a pattern for learning activities. The objectives and their pattern are, however, your best guide. Given these materials (presumably addressing the objectives) and the present competency of the participants, sketch out some ways that the two might get together.

Staff (2)

It is helpful to break your potential staff into two groups: those with special content expertise, and those with skills for assisting the learning process. Process skills include such diverse things as communicating clearly, giving concise effective instructions, helping individuals and groups get down to a task, responding to questions, asking "Socratic" questions, surfacing and resolving conflicts, and showing patience in the face of confusion. Content expertise may be as broad as the general learning objectives or limited to certain specific learning objectives.

The fact that a single learning activity or event may effectively embrace several specific learning objectives is of considerable importance in designing interesting workshops. Economy is a hallmark of good designs. When one complex, unified activity will do the job, don't string the learning out in rigid linear adherence to specific learning objectives. This will bore both staff and participants.

How, then, can your content experts most naturally communicate their expertise, and what are some ways to arrange the pattern of their contributions? According to whether content staff is supplementing the material or the material supplementing staff contributions, by meshing the two sets of potential activities the design starts to take shape.

In considering the staff it remains to sketch supporting roles for the learning process experts. You now have a rough outline for the workshop design. (Note: It is a good practice to have approximately one process staff person for every ten participants when participant interaction is expected to be intense.)

Consultants (3)

Unless they are included for show only, consider consultants as staff and incorporate their contributions in the emerging design above.

Participants (4)

Since completing the needs assessment, you have known the present level of participant expertise. If you haven't done so already, it is time to work in any potential participant contributions and to decide what participants will be doing in their roles as learners. Will they sit passively, staring at your resources, or will they actively engage with them? Add your tentative preferences to the design, but save the details until other elements have been considered.

Methods

A method is a specific, patterned process of interaction among the elements, particularly participants and resources. There are many methods commonly used for adult learning. Review the "Methods Primer" in this chapter and select any methods that seem well calculated to enhance the learning and for which the staff has the requisite skills. If none of the common methods seem quite appropriate for a given learning need, modify them or create new ones. I seldom ever use one in its pristine form. For more details see "Tips on Selecting Methods" in this chapter.

Structure (5)

In considering this element, you begin to add the architectural features to your design. Will staff be up front, milling around, working within groups . . .? Do you want participants in isolation booths, on the floor engrossed in homework back in their rooms, in a big (happy) mass audience, or in smaller groups of some kind? When learning depends on interaction of the participants, groups should probably be no larger than seven to twelve (expert opinions vary). Look for ways to break up larger groups. Your overall guide should be to select structures that are best for the learning. For a more detailed listing of possible structures see "Structures" in this chapter.

Aids (6)

This one is simple: Decide what props are needed for materials, staff, and participants to do what they are supposed to do in the design above. Consult the suggested list provided on page 184 for ideas. Pencil them into the above design and specify how they are to get where they are needed.

Facilities (7)

In the previous activity (selecting resources), you stated some tentative notions regarding desirable facilities. You now have the data to pin it down. How many meeting rooms do you need? Are they available in-house? If so, will they do? Is the learning such that participants should be away from the shop? Out of town? In the country? Would recreation help the learning? Should the environment hold the participants together or disperse them? How comfortable should the rooms be? Many other questions will occur to you. Write your conclusions into the design.

Accommodations (8)

If you have concluded that the workshop should be out of town (a dormitory workshop) as opposed to in town (a commuter workshop), ask some of the same questions you asked about facilities. Anticipate effects on the design and make notes.

Travel (11)

If travel is a factor, it affects starting and ending times. State tentative conclusions now, check them out later.

Time (13)

Which activities should be slow? Which ones fast paced? Some learning needs deliberation; some needs immersion. For example, learning which is centered around the theory of group dynamics will probably occur best when the activities are slowly and deliberately paced. Learning which is centered around the skills required for working with groups will probably occur best when the learner is immersed in fast-paced group exercises.

Estimate the time needed for each activity. Pencil in approximate time blocks. Leave some "white space" for slippage or additions. Allow time at the first of the workshop for climate setting and goal agreement, the activities described in Chapters 10 and 11.

Food and Refreshments (9)

Consider the intensity and length of the activities planned thus far. How many coffee breaks are needed? When? What should be available? How long should they last? Don't be stingy! For most sessions, the constant coffee pot and the "open bathroom door" policy work fine. Note your conclusions in the design.

Energy/Attention

Both of these quantities desert participants and staff alike. In their place come substitutes such as the morning paper, the after-lunch sag, and the four o'clock watch-wind. We have already mentioned the value of refreshments in this regard. In adult education there is another ploy, the *warm-up activity*. (For more information, see p. 147). Warm-ups are particularly handy early in the morning and immediately after lunch. Since you are building in a little flexible white space, impromptu warm-ups can be used to pick up a sagging session. You may now complete time estimates.

Climate

For our purposes, climate does not mean the difference between Minneapolis and Miami; it means the total impact of all the elements on the learning. It is a kind of "workshop weather." The participant's first sniff of it comes with the announcement of the session; it grips him as he is greeted and seated for the learning; and within the first hour, he is either basking in the sunshine or coughing in the cold.

"Climate setting" is an event which occurs at the very outset of the workshop. The climate is a concern throughout the workshop, however, and your success as a forecaster comes from a close rereading of what you have mapped out above.

Your design is now complete.

Dates (10)

Specific dates must wait on further data.

Promotion (12)

Promotion, discussed in Chapter 6, must also wait.

STYLE VARIATIONS

For the extreme authoritarian, designing is an activity for the professional. No amateurs, including other staff, are welcome. The design usually discourages participation and keeps the control "up front." In the moderate position, both designing and the design may include other staff.

For the extreme laissez faire practitioner, designing amounts to meeting with participants (along with any other staff) and saying something like, "What do you want to do in the workshop?" The product *may* be a design. The moderate laissez faire designer would add, "Here are some things you might want to consider. . . ." He might even say, "I don't think that will work." If so, the product may be a lively design.

In the democratic middle, designing is an activity entered into by all possible staff. Participants may also be included. The product is a design that maintains some control "up front" while providing considerable latitude for changes by staff or participants.

SUMMARY

Designing learning activities for adults should be a creative, artistic endeavor. Linear, single-level sequences developed as a "logical" result of the subject matter will not do if interest is to be maintained. The design should be a flexible, complex whole expanding in many directions at once.

***   ***   ***

The remainder of this chapter contains several resources which I have already mentioned, as well as a few others:

> **Tips on Selecting Methods**—cursory
> thoughts on "how to do it."

Methods Primer—a practical exposition of many commonly used methods grouped in a comprehensible fashion.

Warm-up Methods—a separate section for those all-important methods to "get it going."

Tips on Selecting Aids—a collection of my biases.

Structures—a listing of types.

Worksheet Four provides a format for your designs. Three worksheet items require comment:

1. The *Activity* column serves as a quick visual reference for the staff. The short titles recorded here summarize the detailed events in the next column. You should therefore title activites in a manner that will be clear to the staff; no pre-set format titles are implied.

2. The *Events* column provides space for you to describe in as much detail as possible "who," "where," and "how." The details may seem tedious, but they are the only way to assure that staff members are all on the same course. "When" is found in the *Time* column.

3. The *SLO by activity* column is used to reference events according to objectives of the workshop. You may number all SLO's sequentially or by GLO's.

Examples:

SLO #1	GLO 1: SLO #1
SLO #2	SLO #2
SLO #3	SLO #3
SLO #4	
SLO #5	GLO 2: SLO #1
SLO #6	SLO #2

The page following Worksheet Four is a sample design using the worksheet format. No particular writing style is needed in designs. The important thing is to get the details down; writing style is an individual matter.

LEARNING DESIGN

Workshop	Group:	Dates:	Location:

Time	Activity	Events (full description of each step in workshop activities)	SLO #

LEARNING DESIGN

Group:	Adult educators	Dates:	October 4-8	Location:	Austin, Texas

Workshop	The Practice of Adult Education	Events (full description of each step in workshop activities)	SLO #
Time	**Activity**		
AM 9:00	Registration	1. Rosi and Larry alternate greeting participants at door of room as they arrive. Participants are given name tags, pads, and pencils. They are then escorted to one of the four circles of chairs (one in each corner of the room) for small group work. New participants are introduced to any others already seated and invited to help themselves to coffee and donuts found in back of room.	
9:10	Warm-up	2. When all groups are filled, Rosi and Larry go to groups one at a time (Rosi to northwest and northeast corners; Larry, southwest and southeast) and give instructions. Groups are to work for twenty minutes developing a list of statements that describe a "good" adult learning activity. This should be based on each participant's personal experience in such activities. Newsprint and felt markers have been provided for recording list.	SLO #1
		3. After fifteen minutes, Rosi and Larry return to same groups, remind them that there are five minutes remaining, and ask each group to select a spokesperson who will later participate in a panel discussion relating the group's work to the theory of adult education.	
9:30	Climate-Setting	4. Scheduling—Larry asks everyone to move chairs toward center of room to form a "theater in the round." He outlines remainder of morning activities, including invitation to get coffee and go to restrooms whenever they feel the need. Asks for questions and comments (2 minutes).	
		5. Ground rules—Larry briefly states tentative rules. Asks for comments or additions (3 minutes).	
		6. Expectations—Rosi provides each participant with competency model form. She briefly explains that the competencies described on the left side are our restatements of data provided by the participants in response to the mailed needs assessment material, *plus* some of our own ideas. Participants are given three minutes to review. Rosi then asks original groups to reconvene for seven minutes to recommend any changes. Groups report suggested changes. Rosi negotiates final competency model. Total fifteen minutes.	
10:00	Coffee-Break	7. During coffee break, Rosi and Larry caucus to make any needed changes in objectives to be proposed.	
10:15	Need Assessment	8. Larry asks participants to take chairs wherever they like. Explains rating system on model. Asks each participant to self-assess (allows seven minutes). Emphasizes that this is confidential and not an evaluation.	
		9. Larry then asks participants to individually and in their own words state what they need to reach competency. These are written on right side of form and ranked individually (seven minutes). While this is going on, newsprint containing modules is taped to wall.	
10:30	Agreeing on Objectives	10. Larry, pointing to newsprint pages on wall, briefly describes proposed objectives and the learning modules relating to them. Participants are given twenty minutes to mill around, compare the objectives/modules to their individual assessments, and sign up for sessions in which they are interested. At the end of this time, Larry states that the balance of the agenda for the workshop will be built around these choices. The results will be discussed after lunch, and objectives for the workshop will be agreed upon.	
11:00	Panel Discussion	11. Rosi and Larry are joined by group spokesmen in chairs in circle. Two chairs are left vacant in center. Other participants situate themselves as they please. They are invited to join the panel when they have something to say. Larry then begins discussion of theory of adult education by asking each spokesman to report briefly on previous small group work. As appropriate Rosi and Larry add points, and discussion moves in a free form manner. After forty-five minutes, everyone is invited to make summary points. These are recorded on newsprint by Larry. Discuss with participants that no concensus is attempted since one's theory is an individual matter.	SLO #1
12:00 Noon	Lunch		

TIPS ON SELECTING METHODS

The selection of educational methods often has the aura of a witch doctor choosing magic potions. In recent years there has been a deluge of simulations, games, transactional analysis groups, encounter groups (speakeasies), non-verbal exercises (unspeakables), T-groups, and other such learning (or therapy) methods. Both new and experienced practitioners are tempted to keep up with the latest mind-bending methods, and they sometimes go overboard with the current fad. This is not to say that we should not keep up with new developments; nor is it suggested that the selection of methods is not important in the overall scheme of adult education. The important thing to remember is that the requirements of the learning should dictate our selection of methods, not the other way around.

Below are some questions to consider in selecting the appropriate method for a particular learning activity.

1. Is the method suited to the objective?

2. Does it lend itself to knowledge, skill, or attitude learning?

3. Might it yield multiple-learnings, i.e., more than one type?

4. Does it require a greater/lesser degree of background knowledge, skills, or attitudes than participants presently possess?

5. How much time does it take?

6. How much space does it take?

7. What kind of props does it take; are they available?

8. What specialized skills are required of the staff; are they competent in them?

9. Is the method comfortable for the staff; is it consistent with their style?

10. Is the method comfortable for the participants; is it consistent with their expectations?

11. Does the method call for activity or passivity on the part of participants?

12. Does it maintain enough/too much control up front?

13. Is the method slow or fast paced?

14. Does it achieve the objective in the simplest way possible, or is it needlessly showy?

15. What other questions might you add?

METHODS PRIMER

This section serves as an introduction to methods. There are so many methods in use today that it would take several books to describe them. Here some methods are described in enough detail that you can use them without special training. Others are merely sketched in to give you an idea of the possibilities. Since several of these methods require that the educator have special skills, and since you are the best judge of your present level of competency, a *skills rating* is provided to assist you in assessing yourself. Some possible uses of the methods are indicated, as well as the participant activity/passivity implied by each one.

In some cases the groupings suggest derivation, in others merely kinship. The sequence of groups generally moves from methods that require little adultness on the part of the participants to those that require a great deal. Most important, this organizational arrangement is an attempt to span the universe of methods with the economy of ten groups. Not included are certain methods that border on therapy. If you want to add them, they start in Group Eleven. Others (not included) will hopefully fall into one of the ten groups. When you run into new methods, see if you can fit them into this organizational scheme. If not, design your own scheme. The important thing is to have a scheme; without one you may be overwhelmed by the numbers.

The ten groups are:

Group One: Presentations
Group Two: Demonstrations
Group Three: Reading
Group Four: Drama
Group Five: Discussions
Group Six: Cases
Group Seven: Graphics
Group Eight: Playlikes
Group Nine: Gaming
Group Ten: Participant Directed Inquiry

GROUP ONE: PRESENTATIONS

These methods are vehicles for providing information. For the most part they are appropriate only for knowledge learning. When participants lack content background, these methods may serve as the simplest and best way of providing it. They may also put participants to sleep.

1. **Lecture**—a prepared verbal exposition by one speaker before an audience. Though often long, a lecture provides a great deal of information quickly. Requires total participant passivity.

    Skills Rating—speaker should be interesting.

2. **Lecturette**—a short lecture. Puts fewer participants to sleep.
    Skills Rating—requires more discipline than the lecture.

3. **Lecture-Forum**—a lecture followed by the old question/answer period. Provides more activity for participants and gives them a chance to explore selected portions of the content in greater detail.

    Skills Rating—a good traffic cop.

4. **Panel**—a planned conversation before an audience on a selected topic. Usually includes three or more panelists and a leader. Brings more points of view to the content. Participants are passive.

    Skills Rating—leader who is diplomatic.

5. **Panel-Forum**—a panel followed by the habitual question/answer period chaired by the leader. A bit more

participant activity and exploration. Can lead to special interest arguments.

Skills Rating—leader should have some way of organizing the interactions.

6. **Expanding Panel**—a panel with a vacant chair(s). Participants can join in when they feel the call and vacate when they've had their say. Gets unwieldly with groups larger than twenty. Can provide color and a fair amount of participant activity, since even those who don't join in think about it.

Skills Rating—a leader with a solid set of ground rules and the skill to enforce them.

7. **Debate**—an organized argument. Often more intense than the above methods. Control is up front. Participants passive except for hissing and applause.

Skills Rating—low for legislatures, high for law schools.

8. **Presentation**—includes all kinds of "dog and pony shows." Control is up front. Participants passive.

Skills Rating—something more than a desire to "show off."

9. **Films**—presumably for content as well as entertainment. May involve attitude learning as well as knowledge learning. Turning off the lights provides a good opportunity for naps. Participants remain passive unless vicarously involved.

Skills Rating—ability to choose from among many bad films.

10. **Slide Shows**—an addiction of world travelers.

128

11. **Prepared Videotapes** — have an advantage over movies in that lights remain on. Flexible start and stop for discussion purposes. Can make them yourself.

> *Skills Rating*—no particular skills, but you will need a videotape player and sufficient monitors.

12. **Presentation with Listening Teams**—any of the above presentation methods followed by a more organized kind of question/answer period. Before the presentation participants are organized into small groups. Each group is given a listening assignment, e.g., listening for points that are debatable, points that have current applications, etc. At the end of the presentation, the groups caucus and develop questions relating to their particular assignment. The questions are posed to those making the presentation.

> *Skills Rating*—ability to structure assignments that will get at the meat of the presentation.

13. **Presentation with reaction panel**—any of the above presentation methods followed by the reactions of a small, selected group of participants. This participant panel is in effect reacting for the entire group.

> *Skills Rating*—ability to select participants whose views are likely to represent the views of several other participants and the courage to try for a cross-section of views.

GROUP TWO: DEMONSTRATIONS

These methods are vehicles for modeling "correct" techniques or procedures. They are used almost entirely for skills learning. They assume a relative lack of participant proficiency. They may or may not include participant activity.

1. **Demonstration**—an activity in which one or more people "show how it is done." If participants are passive, this method is notoriously ineffective for improving participant skills. The extension service uses it extensively, however, to change attitudes. By demonstrating the profitability of a given procedure, they are effective in gaining an attitude of acceptance from the farmers they serve.
    Skills Rating—the skill to show correct procedure without offending.

2. **Demonstration with Practice**—a demonstration followed by an opportunity for participants to try their hands at it. One of the best means for learning simple skills, provided feedback follows immediately upon completion of the procedure. Without performance feedback, the participant is likely to be reinforced in doing it incorrectly.
    Skills Rating—ability to break procedure down into simple communicable steps. Ability to provide helpful feedback, helpfully. Patience.

3. **Dry Runs**—as nearly as I can make out this is different words for the above method.

4. **Coaching**—providing tips for improving performance. Often follows a demonstration or includes mini-demonstrations as a corrective break in participant performance. Retains all kinds of up front control, to say nothing of power.
    Skills Rating—ability to coach, not grouch. Skill in the assigned procedure.

5. **Rehearsals**—practice just prior to application. May involve practicing a sequence of separately learned simple skills using methods above. Participant active. Control in hands of "director."
    Skills Rating—roughly the same as in coaching. Depending on the activity, may require a "bull-horn" voice.

6. **Drills**—skills practice involving repetition. Sometimes boringly participant active. Unpleasant childhood experiences involving drills may make adults uncomfortable with this method.
    Skills Rating—ability to get participants to try and try again. Sometimes accomplished by telling the *Patient Spider* story.

7. **Puzzles**—an interesting variation in which the skill is not demonstrated but is learned from successfully solving the puzzle. Participants are highly active.
    Skills Rating—benevolence.

8. **Skills Practice Lab**—may be combined with any of the above methods. It involves the formation of small participant groups, often participant selected, for the purpose of practice and mutual feedback.
    Skills Rating—ability to "turn loose" and act only as a resource.

GROUP THREE: READING

These methods are information vehicles. For the most part they are appropriate only for knowledge learning. When participants are lacking in background knowledge, these methods may serve as simple and direct ways of providing it. If participants read the material, they may be active in critiquing it. Up front control is somewhat restricted since "who knows what goes through their heads" while they are reading.

1. **Individual Reading**—a tried and true method by no means outdated.

   > *Skills Rating*—requires skill to select relevant material. Requires reading skill on part of participants.

2. **Read and Discuss**—normally takes the form of a short reading assignment followed by a small group discussion. More participant active than individual reading. More up front control possible if leader is assigned to discussion group.

   > *Skills Rating*—same as above.

3. **Read and Report**—individuals are assigned to read **different** materials and to report the meat of them back to the group. Requires more participant adultness than above methods and greater reading and digesting skills. Up front control is shaky unless leader is prepared to fill in after participant reports.

   > *Skills Rating*—requires skill in getting participants to accept the assignment.

4. **Reading Aloud**—charming.

GROUP FOUR: DRAMA

The methods in this group present information that may often be debated. They are primarily appropriate for knowledge learning, though attitudes may also be involved. These methods may serve as a means of stimulating participant contributions later, or may involve participants in the drama as it is happening.

1. **Skits**—short, rehearsed portrayals that make a point. Often trigger discussion. Participant passive, except for giggles.
   Skills Rating—"ham."

2. **Pantomime**—short, non-verbal portrayals often used in guessing games. Engages participants more than skits. Useful for warm-ups when participants are volunteered as players.
   Skills Rating—ability to keep mouth shut.

3. **Guerrilla Theater**—a contemporary offshoot of the methods above. Works something like jazz in that players normally use a script that describes only basic action and ad-lib the rest. Is noted for getting participants spontaneously caught up in the action.
   Skills Rating—courage and ability to sooth ruffled participants.

GROUP FIVE: DISCUSSIONS

These methods give participants an opportunity to derive information. In a less adult form, they are often used to manipulate assimilation of information. For the most part these methods are appropriate for knowledge learning. In more experienced hands they can also provide a means for attitude learning. The assumption is that participants have something to contribute.

1. **Group Discussion**—an open discussion of a given topic by a relatively small group. May or may not have assigned leader or time limit. Participant active. Appointed group leaders may retain some control.
   Skills Rating—skill in giving instructions that will get discussion going and keep it on target.

2. **Group Buzzes**—usually short discussions of a given topic; set time limit; no leader. Normally relatively small groups of three to five participants. May be quickly formed ("Pick four other people close to you") as more personal divisions of larger groups. Usually groups are asked to report conclusions back to the large group.
   Skills Rating—ability to give clear, crisp instructions.

3. **Brainstorming**—a method of problem solving (or listing) in which group members suggest in rapid-fire order all the possible solutions (or problems) they can think of. Criticism and discussion are ruled out while suggestions are being made. Often has set time limit. Evaluation follows the listing. Intensely participant

active. More ideas and a wider range of ideas than generated by a typical discussion.

> *Skills Rating*—the ability to clearly communicate the ground rules and enforce them. Often requires describing ground rules in detail. May want to state them twice, slowly and distinctly. Ability to give permission to "far out" ideas.

4. **Diagnostic Sessions**—small groups formed for the purpose of diagnosing a problem, situation, process, etc. Ideally, the group should agree on a way of establishing cause/effect relationships, such as looking for evidence, reality-testing, etc.

> *Skills Rating*—ability to help the group establish criteria.

5. **Bull Sessions**—highly informal discussions that often tangentially relate to the learning. The random pattern of discussion often yields new insights and serves to transfer or apply learning more honestly to back home situations. In addition to the numerous sessions that naturally occur, space for them may also be planned into the design. They serve for emotional unwinding.

> *Skills Rating*—if trainer enters in, needs ability to let his hair down and become one of the boys.

GROUP SIX: CASES

The methods in this group provide simulated situations drawn from real life which give the participant an opportunity to apply previously learned knowledge. In use they constitute a kind of test, but one that requires judgement in the application of knowledge rather than simple regurgitation. These methods are highly participant active, but a high degree of up front control may be retained through various means.

1. **Case Study**—an account of a problem situation including sufficient detail to make it possible for groups to analyze the problems involved. The case is a slice of life that invites diagnosis, prescription, and possible treatment. As such it may focus on problem-solving skills as well as knowledge. Up front control is often maintained by loading the dice, i.e., the details of the case lead to correct judgements. Other cases are totally open to differences in judgement. Additional control may be exercised by an assigned leader directing the analysis with "Socratic" questions. There are many packaged cases that can be purchased and used with a little rehearsal. Often, however, they don't fit your needs. In that case, after participating in a few, you can satisfactorily design your own. Simply sit back, take a look at the world around you, and describe a problematic piece of it.

   Skills Rating—requires both knowledge and skill needed to solve the problem. May require the skill to design your own case study. Questioning skills of a Socrates are also useful.

2. **Mini-case**—a case study in miniature; perhaps the most versatile and useful method of all. After a lecture, film, reading, discussion, etc., mini-cases may be used as a quick check on understanding. A good way to do this without putting any single person on the spot is to divide the group into three's, read the mini-case aloud so that all sub-groups can hear, allow subgroups two to five minutes to discuss the problem privately, and then go around the room asking each subgroup to state its conclusions. You should pick up all answers before allowing discussion. You may then reinforce the better answers, or if something crucial was missing from all answers, you can supply it.

In addition, the mini-case may be used in needs assessment (see p. 43), and as an excellent means of practicing the application of certain knowledge (e.g., company policy) to real life situations. For this use it is preferable if the case has no one right response.

> **Example:** "You are conducting a workshop. Participants are all present. The *big chief* was supposed to say his bit at 9:00. It is now 9:20. He has not appeared. Participants are getting restless. *What would you do?*"

As you can see in this example, there are several points to consider: 1) is his "bit" crucial to the learning?, 2) will he be offended if you begin without him?, 3) are participants likely to be negative to the entire workshop as a result of this delay? Judgement is required to respond to the situation; there may be several right answers. From the example, you can see how easy it would be to write your own mini-cases. It is not important that they be true, only that they be plausible.

Skills Rating—anybody can play, provided the
mini-cases are relevant to the
learners' experience.

3. **Critical Incident**—a small piece of a case that states
only the most important or most dramatic transac-
tion.

Example: "Well, you can all eat rotten apples!"
shouted the girls' P.E. teacher as she stormed
out of the faculty meeting. Shortly thereafter, the
music teacher left.

It is then up to the participants to play
detective; to come up with enough information to resolve the conflict or problem. The workshop leader
has all the data but shares it only in response to
direct questions. In this method the **skill** of getting at
the roots of the problem is more important than the
knowledge needed to solve it. This method may be
merrily participant active. Control is exercised by the
structure of the data and the fact that the leader has
it all. In using the method, larger groups can be divided.

Skills Rating—with some of the packaged examples, the skill needed is high. But
for simple, homespun ones, the
beginner can do just fine provided
that the case is not embarrassing
by being too close to the truth.

4. **In-Basket**—a form of the case study in which letters,
memos, phone-messages, etc., are given to the participant playing an assigned role. He is then given time
to write actual responses to the items in his in-basket.
A cast of characters is provided along with a stated

situation, such as "You have been on a business trip. It is Saturday. You decided to drop by the office and spend an hour cleaning off your desk." Each participant is then given an envelope (all envelopes contain the same items) and told that he has one hour to respond in writing to the contents. There are often enough items to provide a time pressure. He is provided with pencil and tablet. After the time has passed, participants form groups to discuss their work. Control can be maintained by assigning a leader to each group.

Skills Rating—knowledge of company policy and ability to critique responses.

GROUP SEVEN: GRAPHICS

The methods in this group are used primarily for warming up and building group cohesion. They involve attitude learning and in some cases knowledge. They are essentially non-threatening but they require a good deal of participant self-direction. They assume no particular knowledge or skills on anyone's part.

1. **Doodling**—the method participants use when they are bored.

2. **Portraits**—rough drawings of the way participants see one another for "getting to know you" activities. Surprisingly, these seldom are embarrassing, and thus require only a modicum of leader skill. Self-portraits are even easier.

    Portraits may also be used as a means of provoking thought. Participants can be asked to *draw* their thoughts on a particular topic. Or they may be asked to draw a picture of their organization, family, etc.

    Skills Rating—the ability to refrain from being an art critic.

3. **Group Paintings**—everyone smears finger paint or tempera on the same paper. Reveals hidden depths and imagine the fun!

    Skills Rating—the ability to recover your dignity.

4. **Group Collage**—similar to the one above, but participants use magazine cutouts and paste.

GROUP EIGHT: PLAYLIKES

These methods allow participants to practice behaviors that involve a complex combination of skills in
situations similar to ones back on the job. Though they
are primarily used for skills practice, they may also be
used for attitude learning. These methods may require a
good deal of adultness on the part of participants and a
great deal of skill and understanding on the part of the
leader. The participant must also have sufficient knowledge to enable him to play-act the behavior. These
methods may employ a variety of structures, such as
diads, triads, and fishbowls (see p. 154).

1. **Role Play**—an unrehearsed, dramatic enactment of a
   response to a situation or human encounter involving
   one or more persons in "playing like." Role play may
   be used for the purpose of situation analysis or to
   provide feedback to the player about his own behavior. They are particularly useful in practicing communication skills when no single right answer will
   measure the attainment of the desired behavior. Participants may either choose or be assigned roles. Roles
   may be written or merely outlined by the leader; they
   may be mostly specified or open to ad-lib.

   Skills Rating—requires skill in getting participants to accept roles, in creating
   a climate of trust, in keeping
   them *doing* rather than *saying*.
   Requires the sensitivity to stop
   the role play when it is threatening, silly, or over-dramatic. Requires the skill to help the group
   process their feelings and to
   provide helpful feedback.

2. **Mini-Role Play**—relates to the role play in the same way as the mini-case related to the case. May also be used in many of the same ways.

   Skills Rating—same as above.

3. **Play Yourself**—commonly role play involves acting out a fictitious person; in this one you play yourself in a fictitious situation but preferably one close to real life. Very useful in practicing skills required back on the job.

   Skills Rating—same as above.

4. **Role Reversal**—you play me, and I play you. And hopefully we gain a bit more respect for each other. Participants need a lot of adultness for this one. Can become hostile. When I see how you see me, I may be shook for weeks.

   Skills Rating—only very experienced practitioners should attempt to use this method.

5. **Mirroring**—while two or more participants engage in a role play, other participants may spontaneously enter in by moving beside one of the players and translating what he *says* into what he *means*. This means that someone in effect plays the part of someone else's alter ego. In this method, participants need a good deal of maturity.

   Skills Rating—very experienced practitioner with a good working knowledge of human psychology.

6. **Movie**—this amounts to the role play of an anticipated situation assisted by a leader who plays movie director, yelling such things as "cut," "roll it," "more _____," or "less _____." Very useful in re-

hearsing workshop leaders, teachers, social workers, personnel interviewers, etc.

Skills Rating—all those described above, plus the willingness to get in there and "bleed" in order to help the participant get it right. You may find yourself crawling on your knees toward the participant saying, "Again . . . Again! **Again!**" And you had best be able to jump to your feet, clap your hands together, and shout, "That's it!" when he does it. And you'd _____ well better mean it!

7. **Videotape Feedback**—taping any of above so that participants may judge their own performance. A very strong method.

Skills Rating—if feedback is limited strictly to that provided by the screen, the leader need not be as skilled as in many of the methods above. If it is to be used more actively, e.g., stopping it to point out particular mannerisms, responses, etc., all the above skills are required.

8. **Social Simulations**—essentially amount to multiple, simultaneous role-plays. They range from very sophisticated packages to loose "general scenes" constructed by the practitioner himself. Either way, written roles and situational details trigger interactions similar to real life.

Skills Rating—good, assertive, fun direction-giving ability. Depending on the simulation other skills may be needed.

GROUP NINE: GAMING

The methods in this group are designed to intensely involve the participant. They are used for knowledge application and skills practice in problem-analysis, decision-making, problem-solving, etc. The intensity is achieved by including a high degree of competition in the learning. Devotees of these methods feel that competition is one of the strongest human drives—whether for good or bad—and that by tapping it, these methods achieve the highest level of experiential learning.

1. **War Games**—ask the Army.

2. **Business Games**—check with Harvard.

3. **Simulation Games**—similar to social simulations but with carefully arranged competitive elements. Gobs of computerized model-building goes into the creation of the games. They are all packaged by professionals. If you want to learn how to design them yourself, you need to spend some time at special workshops planned for this purpose.

   Skills Rating—if you buy a packaged one, you will need to spend days poring over the rules and weeks practicing directing it. The simpler course is to hire a consultant specialized in the particular game that you choose.

GROUP TEN· PARTICIPANT DIRECTED INQUIRY

The purpose of these methods is to involve the participant completely in his own learning. They are highly participant active, retaining no up front control.

1. **Mutual Inquiry**—a group of people sit down without assigned leadership to plan a series of learning activities for their own use, then carry them out. This is the simplest, most adult, and most difficult of all methods.

   Skills Rating—humility based on deep respect for participants.

2. **Learning/Teaching Teams**—the above group with the additional purpose of teaching someone else what they learn.

WARM-UP METHODS

As stated earlier, warm-ups are essential in the morning and right after lunch. Though they tend to be fun (even gamey), they should be in some way related to the objectives of the learning.

For short workshops (one day or less) warm-ups should last no longer than ten or fifteen minutes; for long workshops (when the group will be together for many days) warm-ups may need to last an hour or more, particularly the first day.

I do not intend to spell out methods for your use. Rather, you should use the ingredients described here to "mix up" your own. These are the best warm-ups.

Ingredients:

1. Sign-board materials for hanging from the neck and advertising yourself. May contain information like:
   "When I smell onions, I _____"
   "On my way to the workshop _____"
   "When I am in a new group _____"
   "What I expect from this workshop
       is _____"
   "I am happiest when _____"

2. Art materials for expressing self in some of the following ways:

   Group Drawings
   Group Paintings
   Collages
   Life-Story Comic Strips
   Peak-Experience Doodles

147

3. Items for participant exploration include:

Eggs   Lemon slices
Oranges   Pillows or cushions
Sand/Salt   Coffee cups

4. Body exercises like:

Deep breathing
Tensing/relaxing muscles
Stretching
Tapping all over head with finger tips

5. Private fantasy suggestions such as:

"Someone is calling your name . . ."
"Think of yourself floating in space . . ."
"Make yourself tiny and enter your
    own body . . ."
"You are standing in front of a cave . . ."

6. Controversial topics like:

"Marriage should be abolished."
"Should the oil industry be nationalized?"
"Should movies be censored?"
"The _____ liberation move-
    ment is a lot of hooey."

7. Topics for which participants may propose a theory
   or philosophy, such as:

Adult education   Social work
Good management   Civic work
Good teaching

8. Group project assignments based on:

  Tinker-toy architecture
  Puzzles of all kinds

9. Objects for participants to consider in inventing short games which they then play. Such objects are:

  Balls   Cards
  Jacks   Paper
  Matches

10. Pantomime assignments in which some participants act out and some guess. Complex ones are best, for example:

  Riding on a ferris wheel
  Riding on a roller coaster
  Strolling by the local river, lake, park, etc.
  Eating artichokes
  Asking for a raise

11. Information cards for participants to use in milling and matching.

  Index cards containing questions, one of a matched pair

  Index cards containing answers, the other part of a matched pair

  A referee

There they are. They can be combined in all sorts of fascinating ways. Have fun!

149

TIPS ON SELECTING AIDS

Many of the aids used in workshops are gimmicks. And the more mechanical they are, the less I like them. As you can see, I really am going to tell you some of my biases. Aids should be selected for their value in assisting the learning, not for their PR value or for "looking good." You may accept or reject my tips, but here they are.

1. Films require projectors. Projectors require extension cords. People trip on extension cords, and cords come unplugged. Projectors also require bulbs. Bulbs blow. Even with spare bulbs, it takes time to change them. Bulbs project images on a screen. For images to be seen, lights must be lowered. Lowered lights put overworked adults to sleep. Why bother?

2. Blackboards are messy. They often make adults feel like children. Use newsprint instead. Easels are nice if sturdy, but you can simply tape or tack newsprint to the wall or hang it over George Washington's picture. Dark-colored felt-tip pens show up much better on newsprint than chalk does on blackboards.

3. Masking tape is a must.

4. Pencils are better than pens if a sharpener is available.

5. Legal size tablets are (were) cheap and serve as well as notebooks. Notebooks are needed when papers are to be kept together after the session. When notebooks are provided, a paper punch is essential.

6. Videotapes are better than films. They are more flexible and do not require lowered lights. Because they are machines, they require a trial run prior to the session.

7. Pointers should be aimed at the chart, not at people. If you use a pointer, check to see if participants are sitting on their fingers.

8. Overheads require projectors, etc. Flipcharts don't. Use overheads only when size of group produces the need to see from a distance.

9. Tape recorders may make people up-tight.

10. Tinker toys are fun!

11. Mikes produce distance. Use only when distance is a necessary result of large audiences. Otherwise learn how to use your voice.

12. Lecterns are to lean on. Are you that feeble? By definition, they mean that you have the authority and the participants have none. Perhaps acceptable for speeches from which no one is supposed to learn.

13. Name tags are a bother but often needed. They aid in calling people by name. They help eliminate phrases like "you people."

14. Copying machines nearby are a real help.

15. Water pitchers, glasses, and ashtrays are considerate.

16. Coffee (for me) is essential.

Well, there they are. You can probably get a decent price for that projector.

STRUCTURES

Following is a list of some of the forms around which learning activity is built; the ingredients of its architectural superstructure. As such, they suggest ways in which participants and learning resources may be combined and arranged to support learning activities. These are by no means all possible structural forms; feel free to add to the list.

Individual Structures

> An individual:
> on a chair
> behind a table
> on the floor
> facing a speaker
> facing a participant
> facing a book
> facing a programmed text
> isolated in an audience
> looking out the window
> back in his room
> in consultation with staff

Small Group Structures

More and more, small groups are becoming the main structure for serious adult learning. Large groups are being relegated to entertainment and public relations. It is usually possible to break large groups into small ones for more effective interaction while learning. Here are some small group structures.

1. **Diads**—participant pairs

2. **Triads**—participant threesomes

3. **Quadrads**—may be formed from two diads

4. **Etc.**—on up to twelve participants

5. **Fishbowls**—participants seated in a circle around some learning activity, such as a role-play

6. **Group-on-group**—one group surrounded by another; the second group often observes the first

7. **Circles**—a group seated in a circle

8. **Squares**—a group seated in a square

9. **Table groups**—a group around a table

10. **Competing groups**—breaking larger groups into competing sub-groups

11. **Collaborating groups**—as above

13. **Lines**—small groups in a line

Staff Structures

1. **Up front**—staff in front (or center) of room

2. **Within groups**—providing content or facilitating the learning process

3. **Available**—staff members available to groups (or individuals) for consultation or facilitation

4. **Now-you-see-them/now-you-don't** — staff members who do their bits and split, leaving no time for questions

5. **Out front**—staff acting as hosts/hostesses

6. **In back**—staff observing the process for the purpose of providing feedback to group(s) or up-front staff

7. **Faculty**—individual staff members conducting separate sessions simultaneously

BUDGETING 5

As stated earlier in this book, budgeting is the "how of the how." It is a cloud that hangs over authoritarian, laissez faire, and democratic practitioners alike. As presented here, budgeting is an activity that occurs after you have assessed needs, specified objectives, and designed learning activities to meet them. To be sure, the process should not be begun if there is no assurance of the funds to carry it out, but neither should the budget dictate needs, objectives, and activities. In planning workshops, the best budgeting procedure is to make decisions based on the dictates of the required learning; *then* determine if you can afford them. In essence, this is a budgeting-by-objectives approach.

At this point, you have made decisions about four things:

1. What needs to be learned

2. What specific learning results are expected

3. What resources are needed for the learning

4. How the learning can best occur

You must determine now, as precisely as possible, what these decisions are going to cost, and whether or not you can raise the cash to pay for them. There are eight steps involved in doing this:

1. Make cost estimates of all items required by the proposed plan.

2. Add them.

3. List all available funds, i.e., those from organizations, from foundations, grants, and from the participants.

4. Add these.

5. Subtract funds needed for future activities, if any. The remaining sum is the amount available for the workshop.

6. Compare no. 2 with no. 5.

7. If no. 5 is greater than no. 2, proceed.

7. If no. 2 is greater than no. 5, consider alternatives that will still meet the objectives.

8. Add some frills or save for a rainy day.

8. If no affordable alternatives can be found, send regrets and scrap the workshop.

CONSIDERING ALTERNATIVES

It is no fun at all to scrap a workshop after this much work. If there is a shortage of money you should probably take step no. 7 very seriously. Besides, in this world of competing needs it is always a good practice to consider alternatives when money is involved. As a means of discovering potential alternatives, the standard list of elements in Chapter 3 may be used.

1. Materials

Are there materials that will substitute for those presently in the design and still get the job done? Are there less expensive uses of the same materials, e.g., summaries of a book's contents rather than the book itself? Will a carefully designed role-play or simulation do as well (or better) than the film originally selected? Can the sophisticated packaged materials be replaced with some you design yourself?

2. Workshop Staff

Even in-house people who are not paid from workshop funds are charged to somebody's budget. If it is too expensive for a supervisor to allow his people to act as workshop staff, is there someone else who could serve? Could you make do with a smaller staff? Could you involve participants in leadership roles to take the place of certain staff? Could you use three panelists instead of five?

3. Consultants

Did you select a consultant for any reason other than those listed in Chapter 3? If so, there is still time to "deselect." It is not wise to ask consultants to lower their fees.

4. Participants

Can you be more restrictive about who attends? Or conversely, can you attract more participants who will pay? Can you employ a learning method that will draw more from participants and require less from other resources?

5. Structure

Can you rearrange groupings to cut down on required space? Can you stagger group and individual work so that fewer rooms will be required? If you really must, can you find some way to use larger groups effectively?

6. Aids

Do you really need those prepared graphics; would crude newsprint drawings do as well? Is the overhead for looking good or for good looking? Could simple tablets replace the specially bound participant packets?

7. Facility

Is there an adequate facility less posh, closer, etc.?

8. Accommodations

Can participants pick up their own tabs? Can it be a commuter workshop? Would barracks do?

160

9. Food and Refreshments

Can participants buy their own meals or bring sack lunches? Having participants chip in for refreshments is usually very disturbing to the learning climate; the workshop should either provide refreshments or allow participants sufficient time to go somewhere and buy their own.

10. Dates

Will you have more cash on hand if you change dates? Is that perfect facility less expensive in the off-season? Can you shorten the workshop?

11. Travel

How about car-pooling? Can you use a chartered bus? Can you stay in town?

12. Promotion

Do you really need the five-color brochure, could you get adequate results with a more interesting format, shape, or arrangement? Can you drop one of the mailings? Can you mail only to the top people?

13. Timing

Can you move some of the learning at a faster pace, shortening the workshop? Can you use night sessions? Can you leave some of the learning for back on the job?

Many of these alternatives will require redesigning. Consequently, while the requirements of the learning are

161

your primary guide, you should keep one eye on the budget while designing in the first place. If redesign is necessary, you must balance its costs with the savings of the alternative.

***   ***   ***

Worksheet 5, *Budgeting*, follows in this chapter.

The worksheet is broken into two major sections, *Funds* and *Costs*. The vertical subtotal column provides space for line item totals within the major sections; the total column provides for the comparison of funds to costs. In figuring staff costs, you may record living expenses in the per diem space in the staff subsection. You may optionally compute and record staff and participant costs in the same manner when that cost is not paid directly from the budget but is still a factor because time is being taken away from other work. When that data is recorded, the total does not appear in the subtotal (actual cash) column but may be added to the total cash cost to provide the complete cost of the workshop.

Staff travel is recorded with participant travel; consultant travel becomes part of the total consultant cost. Space is provided to record cost of participant accommodations when paid directly, or alternately to compute cost of per diem when that method is chosen. Travel cost may be estimated by averaging typical costs from selected locations.

A revised budget worksheet is prepared as *actual* rather than estimated costs are known. This provides you with a running account of where you stand in relation to money.

WORKSHOP BUDGET

Workshop	Group

		SUBTOTALS	TOTALS
FUNDS			
Available			
1. From Organization(s)	$ _____		
2. From Foundations or contracts	$ _____		
3. From participants	$ _____	$	
Required for Future Activities			
1. _____	$ _____		
2. _____	$ _____		
3. _____	$ _____	$	$

COSTS

1. Materials

		SUBTOTALS
a) _____	$ _____	
b) _____	$ _____	
c) _____	$ _____	
d) _____	$ _____	$

2. Staff (if paid from your budget)

Name	Time	Amount	Per diem	=	
a) _____	_____	$ _____	$ _____	$ _____	
b) _____	_____	$ _____	$ _____	$ _____	
c) _____	_____	$ _____	$ _____	$ _____	
d) _____	_____	$ _____	$ _____	$ _____	$

Staff (optional method)

No.	x	Time from job	x	Avg. rate	=	
_____		_____		_____		$ _____

3. Consultants

Name	Total fee	Per diem	Travel	=	
a) _____	$ _____	$ _____	$ _____	$ _____	
b) _____	$ _____	$ _____	$ _____	$ _____	
c) _____	$ _____	$ _____	$ _____	$ _____	
d) _____	$ _____	$ _____	$ _____	$ _____	$

4. Participants (optional)

No.	x	Time from job	x	Avg. rate	=	
_____		_____		_____		$ _____

5. Structure   N/A

6. Aids

Description	Quantity	
_____	_____	$ _____
_____	_____	$ _____
_____	_____	$ _____
_____	_____	$ _____
_____	_____	$ _____
_____	_____	$ _____
_____	_____	$ _____
_____	_____	$ _____
_____	_____	$ _____
_____	_____	$ _____
_____	_____	$ _____
_____	_____	$

7. Facility

a) Meeting rooms	$ _____	
b) Staff work rooms	$ _____	
c) Hospitality suite	$ _____	
d) Tips	$ _____	
e) Other	$ _____	$

163

8. Accommodations (if paid directly by workshop)

Number	Room type	Rate	
		$	$
		$	$
		$	$
		$	$
		$	$

OR

Per diem (if flat rate for all participants)

Number	Rate	
	$	$
	$	$
	$	$

Staff Accommodations (if paid directly)

Number	Room type	Rate	
		$	$
		$	$
		$	$ $

9. Food and Refreshments (paid directly)

a) Catered meals (B, L, D)

	No. served	Cost	Tip	
		$	$	$
		$	$	$
		$	$	$
		$	$	$
		$	$	$

b) Refreshments

Type	Quantity	Cost	Tip	
		$	$	$
		$	$	$
		$	$	$
		$	$	$
		$	$	$ $

10. Dates   N/A

11. Travel (for participants and staff if paid directly)

Mode	Number	(Estimate)	
		$	
		$	
		$	
		$	
		$	$

12. Promotion

Item	Number		
		$	
		$	
		$	
		$	
		$	$ $

Surplus or shortage (+ or —) $

164

MAKING ARRANGEMENTS 6

Now the fun begins! After countless hours of talking, listening, guessing, strategizing, and calculating, you can finally begin to spend the money. At this point, I always feel a little like a third grader buying school supplies. But this job can be drudgery if you insist on acting grown up. For instance, you might turn your graphics entirely over to the art department rather than doodling around with the artists and learning their colorful language. You might order your books by phone rather than going over to the bookstore and browsing while you place your order. You might have a business-like telephone conversation with the hotel business office rather than taking a little vacation, complete with a VIP tour of the facility. You might send a very crisp announcement to participants rather than describing some of the fun you have cooked up.

However you do it, you are concerned here with details—with dotting the "i's." Thoroughness in making arrangements is easily measured; you simply observe the number of unforeseen hassles that occur. If events flow smoothly and interruptions to the learning are at a minimum, the workshop planner has done a good job.

As a way of organizing details and making certain that none of them slide unnoticed off the scratch pad, the standard list of elements is a ready-made worry-saver. Worksheet 6 is provided for recording necessary data about these elements. Instructions for the use of the worksheet and supporting documents are included in the text in bold type for visual convenience. Many of the blanks on the worksheet are described in following chapters.

1. Materials

You know what you want and how much you can spend; place those orders—NOW! Books on order can take six weeks or more to arrive, films often require two or three months advance reservation. If articles are to be written, summaries prepared, and copies made, the sooner the better. Nothing can be more nerve-racking than scrambling for educational materials the day before the workshop.

In the materials section of the worksheet, the "Date Needed" should be a date that allows sufficient time for staff review and preparation; other items are self-explanatory. When all materials are on hand check the blocks marked "Arranged."

2. Staff

If you are borrowing staff from other departments, make a formal request through channels. If you don't have approval on paper, you don't have approval. If other staff members have not been previously involved in planning, it is time to bring them in. This includes a briefing on problems, needs, and objectives; a thorough presentation of the design; a review of the materials to be used; and a discussion of how each person on the staff fits in. With this as background, team members are ready to start preparing themselves for their parts. It is probably a good idea to end this staff meeting by setting a date for the rehearsal (see Chapter Seven).

> In the "Staff" section of the worksheet the special assignments spaces are for later use. Check the "arranged" block for each staff person when all described above is complete. Enter the date of the scheduled rehearsal in the blank indicated.

3. Consultants

Consultants are a lot of bother. If they are good, they are often booked for eons into the future; if they are not booked that far ahead, they may not be good. This is actually an exaggeration. Consultants often use the full calendar routine as a means of selecting the most exciting assignments. It's amazing how a good fee makes any assignment more exciting. At any rate, when you are planning workshops, book consultants well in advance.

Assuming that you checked consultant availability when you were selecting resources, you should call again (person-to-person), discuss the details of the assignment and compensation, review possible dates, and secure a commitment. **Record date committed on worksheet.** Once a final date has been set, formalize this telephone conversation with a written agreement. This can often take the form of a simple business letter—**record in "Date Contract Sent"**—followed by a written response from the consultant which closes the contract. At a minimum this agreement should contain the following data:

a) Amount of consultant time required

b) Dates

c) Specific activities expected of the consultant

d) Specific (if possible) times for his performance

e) Travel arrangements (if made by workshop planner)

f) Accommodations, either already arranged or available for the consultant's selection

g) The time and place for a rehearsal before his performance

h) A clear statement of his fee, per diem, and travel allowance

When a written response from the consultant is received, check the "Arranged" blocks.

4. Participants

If prospective participants are all in-house, it may now be possible to prepare a roster. If so, the roster will provide valuable data for several other arrangements. **In this case we may mark the "arranged" block.** If not, you must at least do a random check for potential dates and make an estimate of the number of participants expected to attend. **This number is entered in the "Number Estimated" blank and the "Arranged" block is checked.** If you know that there will be great demand, it is good practice to limit enrollment on a first-come-first-served basis to the number contemplated in the design. If cancellations occur, you may accept others by preparing a waiting list.

5. Structure

Nothing more to do at this point. **This data is completed at a point described in a later chapter.**

6. Aids

It is time to begin preparing aids. Like materials, aids often require lead time. Particularly important are the content aids, e.g., prepared charts, graphs, overhead plates, etc. Equipment rental usually requires less lead time if you know your sources. Pencils, notepads, and other consumable supplies are usually easy to obtain. (See "Aids Inventory" for possibilities.)

> **Enter "Description," "Quantity," and "Order Date" on the worksheet. The "Room No./Time" blanks are completed in the setting-up stage. When all aids are on hand, check the "Arranged" blocks.**

7. Facilities

This is the big one at this stage of planning. Workshops, otherwise well-planned, can fall apart due to inadquate facilities planning. By now, you have decided if the workshop will be held in-house, in town, or out of town; you also know how much space is needed, what kind, and how much you can spend for facilities. Your task now involves comparative shopping, review of possible dates, decision-making, and nailing down detailed arrangements (this involves a procedure similar to the one described for consultants). It is not possible to overemphasize the impact of environment on learning; the walls themselves act as teachers.

It should be stressed that this is to be a learning environment for adults. Grammar school chairs produce a hangover; neat, bolted-down rows, a dread. The smell of oiled floors may inspire nostalgia, but adult expectations lift at the smell of carpet cleaning fluid. Blackboarded walls may look like learning, but warm-walled rooms lead to greater exchange. I could go on, but you get the idea.

As a means of organizing facility arrangements, let's break the problem into smaller pieces:

a. *Commuter workshop facilities*—include in-house facilities, other free local facilities, and paid local facilities. In-house facilities are usually the least desirable for adult learning. Other free in-town facilities often present tight scheduling problems and cranky rules. In-town paid facilities usually allow more demand of the space.

b. *Dormitory workshop facilities*—include retreat facilities in the country and facilities in other cities which may offer enhanced recreational opportunities. Both types are usually paid for and should provide better elements for adult learning.

For a more detailed analysis, see "Facilities Survey," a form to be used in surveying potential facilities.

> The "Surveys Complete" blanks are for names of facilities being surveyed. Set a target date for making a selection. Enter "Written Request Date" and "Confirmation Date." The "Room No./Time" and "Equipment Required" blanks are for data from the agreement. The agreement (contract) should be attached. The blank by "Facility" is for the name of the one selected. When the contract is secure, check the "Arranged" blocks.

8. Accommodations

If this is to be a dormitory workshop, make at least tentative arrangements for accommodations. You should usually attempt to arrange for accommodations in the same building or complex in which the workshop will be held, although to provide enough rooms you may have to use additional establishments. At this point you should specify the relative luxury and expense of the rooms or provide a range from which participants can select. You also need to specify the approximate number of single, double/one bed, and double/two bed rooms needed.

171

As an attachment to the "Facilities Survey," you will find a form for your use in surveying potential accommodations (p183). Included in this form are some thirty items. In checking these items, good common sense is your best guide. Occasionally however you may be blinded by some new wave of romanticism. In recent years, one such wave has been the "compassionate" desire to get participants away from telephones. That is also a good way to keep them away from the workshop. Participants grow irritated at slapping mosquitoes while standing in line by the phone booth. In one extreme case, I found myself sleeping by a patio pay phone expecting at any minute *the call* from my wife that would send me racing for the delivery room thirty miles away. So cut the "schmaltz," twentieth century adults are addicted to amenities, and they don't learn well without them.

If participants are known by name, you may proceed to make firm room reservations, giving the hotel or other establishments a roster indicating price preferences, pairings, etc., for each participant. If participants' names or numbers are not known, you must estimate the number, type, and luxury of rooms needed and arrange for a certain number to be held until a specified date when firm reservations can be concluded. The contract procedure described for consultants may again be used.

> The spaces on Worksheet 6 are completed as they are for the "Facility" section. Begin now, revise as results from promotion become clearer. When the contract is secure, check the "Arranged" block.

9. Food and Refreshments

You have already calculated the times and dimensions of the feasting; you know how much participants are providing for themselves and how much the workshop is providing. You must now make firm arrangements for all meals and refreshments to be provided by the workshop. In paid facilities there is often a requirement that the facility supply and serve any refreshments; violate such rules only at the risk of bad "vibes" surrounding the learning climate. In free facilities, you must usually arrange independently for food and refreshments. For more detail, see "Facilities Survey." For food and refreshments provided by the facility, the contract should include the details. If other arrangements are made, the procedure described for contracting with consultants should again be used.

> The blanks on the worksheet are completed in the same manner as those for "Facilities" and "Accommodations." The "Room No./Time" blanks may not be completed until the setting-up stage, Chapter 9. When all arrangements are secure, check the "Arranged" blocks.

10. Dates

By now you should know the relative availability of workshop staff, consultants, participants, facilities, and accommodations (if applicable). You should glance next at the availability of travel and the implications it may have for dates. With breath held, you then attempt to select the dates which match the greatest number of "availabilities"; seldom do they all coincide. After selecting the best possible dates, decide if the workshop will still work given scheduling conflicts. Add this firm date to all arrangements above, or drop back and punt.

> The worksheet provides space for four potential dates. Review other data on the worksheet and check the indicated ( )'s if potential dates are acceptable for the indicated elements. The date receiving the greatest number of checks is selected and entered in the "Selected" blank. Then check the "Arranged" block.

11. Travel

If possible, leave participant travel arrangements to participants. Take responsibility only for your own travel and perhaps that of other staff and consultants. An exception to this is chartered transportation. If despite the warning you still choose to make individual arrangements for participants, you are on your own. If participants handle their own transportation, you might provide them with schedules and information about cabs, limousines, and parking facilities. Whatever your responsibility for travel arrangements, now is the time to choose modes and make reservations.

> The "Arrival Time" blanks are for the purpose of coordination. When reservations are secure, check the "Arranged" blocks.

12. Promotion

You are ready to advertise the workshop! There are any number of ways to do this, including in-house memos, telephone calls, newspaper/radio/television announcements, posted notices, or direct mailing. In my experience, direct mail or telephone contact is best since it is more personal. Whatever the method, it is important that the invitation be interesting and complete. At a minimum, it should include the following information:

- Needs addressed by the workshop and method of arriving at them
- Objectives
- General methodology
- Data on staff and consultants indicating their expertise and experience
- Location
- Dates
- Agenda (may be general, indicating only times for major sessions)
- Fees, if any
- Method of registering
  1) at the workshop—time, place, etc.
  2) pre-registering—address, telephone number, deposits, etc.

It may also include information regarding:

- Accommodations
- Food
- Recreation
- Suggested attire
- Transportation
- Maps
- Suggested preparation such as reading, taking out insurance, etc.

Once you decide what to include, you must have the promotional material prepared and on its way as soon as possible (like yesterday). If participants are unknown, the completion of many of the above arrangements will await their response. If affordable, it often pays to follow the initial announcement with a reminder approximately two weeks before the workshop.

The "Medium Description" is for recording the various promotional means you may choose. The "Preparation Target Date" is for anything requiring preparation. The "1st Contact Date" records mailing or phoning done at this time. When complete, check the "Arranged" blocks.

Worksheet 6 is found on the following page. It is to be added to your "Workshop Staff Packet." It is designed so that it may also serve for several other activities to be described in the next three chapters of this book. In addition, I have included a "Facility Survey," complete with the "Accommodations Survey" attachment for dormitory (residential) workshops. Finally, the "Aids Inventory" is for your use in reviewing possible aids and selecting those needed for the workshop.

ARRANGEMENTS
(Complete in pencil)

Workshop

This worksheet is used for arranging, rehearsing, packing, and setting up.

Arranged / Rehearsed / Packed / Set

1. MATERIALS

Description	Quantity	Date Ordered	Date Needed

Problems

2. STAFF

Rehearsal Date _____

Name	Date Requested	Date Approved	Special Assignments

Problems

3. CONSULTANTS

Name	Date Committed	Date Contract Sent	Rehearsal Date

Problems

4. PARTICIPANTS (Invitation/response list attached)

No. Estimated: _____   Preregistration no. _____   Final No. _____

Problems

5. STRUCTURE

Sketch attached

Room #/Time	# Tables	# Chairs	Other Furniture	
				( )
				( )
				( )
				( )
				( )

Problems

178

Arranged / Rehearsed / Packed / Set

6. AIDS (See "Aids Inventory" for ideas)   Inventory attached ( )

Description   Quantity   Order Date   Room #/Time

Problems

7. FACILITY _____ (Details on attached survey)

Surveys Complete   Facility selection target date   Written Request Date   Confirmation Date
_____( )
_____( )
_____( )

Room #/Time   Equipment Required

Agreement attached ( )

Problems

8. ACCOMMODATIONS (1) _____
                   (2) _____   (Details on attached survey)

Surveys Complete   Selection Target Date   Written Request Date   Confirmation Date
_____( )
_____( )

Problems

9. FOOD & REFRESHMENTS (Additional information on Facility Survey)

Description   Quantity   Written request date/caterer   Confirmation date   Room #/Time

Problems

179

10. DATES

Selected _____

Potential Dates	Staff	Consultants	Participants	Facilities	Accom.	Travel
	( )	( )	( )	( )	( )	( )
	( )	( )	( )	( )	( )	( )
	( )	( )	( )	( )	( )	( )
	( )	( )	( )	( )	( )	( )

Problems

11. TRAVEL

Name	Mode	Date	Arrival time

Problems

12. PROMOTION (For results, see participants)

Medium Description	Preparation Target Date	1st Contact Date	2nd Contact Date

Problems

180

FACILITY SURVEY

REQUIREMENTS

Workshop:

No. Participants _____ No. Meeting Rooms _____

Size	Times
_____	_____
_____	_____
_____	_____

Other requirements

SURVEY DATA

Facility Name _____   Address _____

Contact _____   Telephone _____

AVAILABILITY

Dates	Times	No. Meeting Rooms	Acceptable
_____	_____	_____	( )
_____	_____	_____	( )
_____	_____	_____	( )

				Yes	No
COSTS	$_____	Tips? _____	Affordable	( )	( )

ACCESSIBILITY

PARKING (Free or fee?)

OVERALL QUALITY

OTHER COMMENTS

EQUIPMENT   Available (✓)

Chalkboards	( )	Projectors	( )	P.A. system	( )	Water pitchers	( )
Easels	( )	_____	( )	Mikes	( )	Glasses	( )
Screen	( )			Adequate tables	( )	Ash trays	( )
Lecterns	( )	Tape player	( )	Adequate chairs	( )	Cups	( )
_____	( )	_____	( )	_____	( )	_____	( )
_____	( )	_____	( )	_____	( )	_____	( )

REFRESHMENT NEEDS   Check (✓) where appropriate

Catered / Costs (incl. tips)

Coffee	( )	$_____	Cokes	( )	$_____
Water	( )	$_____	Ice	( )	$_____
Tea	( )	$_____	Booze	( )	$_____
_____	( )	$_____	_____	( )	$_____
_____	( )	$_____	_____	( )	$_____

We must provide

Coffee	( )	Sugar	( )	Ice	( )
Water	( )	Cream	( )	Booze	( )
Tea	( )	Cups	( )	Mixers	( )
Cokes	( )	Glasses	( )	_____	( )
_____	( )	_____	( )	_____	( )

FOOD   Catered

	Caterer	Costs (incl. tips)
B	_____	$_____
L	_____	$_____
D	_____	$_____

Not Catered

Restaurants in Area		Est. Cost to Participant
Convenience _____	B	$_____
Speed _____	L	$_____
Variety _____	D	$_____
Quality _____		

ASSORTED NEEDS

Telephones _____   Copy machine _____

Messages _____   Restroom convenience _____

Others _____   Cleanup arrangements _____

MEETING ROOMS Acceptable (✓) Unacceptable (x)

| | No or name | Size | Seating Capacity | Appearance |

1. _____ _____ ( ) _____ ( ) _____ ( )

Convenience to other rooms _____( )

Entrance/exit adequate _____( ) Noise level_____( )

Heating/air cond. ( ) Elec. outlets ( ) Lighting ( ) Darkening drapes ( )
Ventilation/smoke ( ) Windows ( ) Carpets ( ) Room height ( )

Room flexibility _____ ( )

Furniture movability _____( )

MEETING ROOMS Acceptable (✓) Unacceptable (x)

| | No or name | Size | Seating Capacity | Appearance |

1. _____ _____ ( ) _____ ( ) _____ ( )

Convenience to other rooms _____( )

Entrance/exit adequate _____( ) Noise level_____( )

Heating/air cond. ( ) Elec. outlets ( ) Lighting ( ) Darkening drapes ( )
Ventilation/smoke ( ) Windows ( ) Carpets ( ) Room height ( )

Room flexibility _____ ( )

Furniture movability _____( )

MEETING ROOMS Acceptable (✓) Unacceptable (x)

| | No or name | Size | Seating Capacity | Appearance |

1. _____ _____ ( ) _____ ( ) _____ ( )

Convenience to other rooms _____( )

Entrance/exit adequate _____( ) Noise level_____( )

Heating/air cond. ( ) Elec. outlets ( ) Lighting ( ) Darkening drapes ( )
Ventilation/smoke ( ) Windows ( ) Carpets ( ) Room height ( )

Room flexibility _____ ( )

Furniture movability _____( )

MEETING ROOMS Acceptable (✓) Unacceptable (x)

| | No or name | Size | Seating Capacity | Appearance |

1. _____ _____ ( ) _____ ( ) _____ ( )

Convenience to other rooms _____( )

Entrance/exit adequate _____( ) Noise level_____( )

Heating/air cond. ( ) Elec. outlets ( ) Lighting ( ) Darkening drapes ( )
Ventilation/smoke ( ) Windows ( ) Carpets ( ) Room height ( )

Room flexibility _____ ( )

Furniture movability _____( )

MEETING ROOMS Acceptable (✓) Unacceptable (x)

| | No or name | Size | Seating Capacity | Appearance |

1. _____ _____ ( ) _____ ( ) _____ ( )

Convenience to other rooms _____( )

Entrance/exit adequate _____( ) Noise level_____( )

Heating/air cond. ( ) Elec. outlets ( ) Lighting ( ) Darkening drapes ( )
Ventilation/smoke ( ) Windows ( ) Carpets ( ) Room height ( )

Room flexibility _____ ( )

Furniture movability _____( )

182

ACCOMMODATIONS SURVEY

REQUIREMENTS

Workshop:

No. Participants _____ No. Rooms _____

Type	No.	Price range
Single/1 bd.	_____	$ _____
Double/1 bd.	_____	$ _____
Double/2 bd.	_____	$ _____
Suites	_____	$ _____

Other requirements

SURVEY DATA

Establishment   Address

Contact   Telephone

DATES (Possible dates for sufficient rooms)   _____ _____
                                                  _____ _____

ROOMS

Types	No. available	Price range	No. reserved
a) Single/1 bd.	_____	$ _____ to $ _____	_____
b) Double/1 bd.	_____	$ _____ to $ _____	_____
c) Double/2 bd.	_____	$ _____ to $ _____	_____
d) Suites	_____	$ _____ to $ _____	_____

Proximity To Meeting (describe)

No. rooms   Proximity

_____   _____
_____   _____
_____   _____

Rooms Generally

[(✓) Acceptable   (x) Unacceptable]

Appearance ( )	Bed comfort ( )	Telephones ( )	Tem. control ( )
Restrooms ( )	Closet space ( )	TV ( )	Lighting ( )
Cleanliness ( )	Noise insulation ( )	Reading chair ( )	Desk ( )

Reservation Policy

Late Check-Out Policy

OTHER

Convenience of:
- Entertainment _____
- Recreation _____
- Food _____
- Liquor laws _____

Special Attractions

Description   Dates

_____   _____
_____   _____

Services (describe)

- Laundry _____
- Medical _____
- Messages _____

AIDS INVENTORY

CONTENT AIDS

Need

1. Printed Materials
( ) books
( ) articles
( ) summaries
( ) other_____
2. Prepared Visuals:
( ) flip charts
( ) posters
( ) overhead plates
( ) slides
( ) films
( ) video cassettes
( ) other_____
3. Prepared Audio:
( ) tapes
( ) records
( ) other _____

Need

4. Equipment
( ) overhead projector
( ) movie projector
( ) slide projector
( ) tape player
( ) record player
( ) video tape player
( ) other_____
5. Packaged Materials:
( ) games
( ) simulations
( ) programmed learning
( ) other_____
6. Demonstration Materials:
( ) models
( ) tinker-toys
( ) other _____

STAFF AIDS

Need
( ) blackboard
( ) chalk
( ) erasers
( ) newsprint pads
( ) felt pens
( ) easels
( ) cork board
( ) flannel board
( ) magnetic board
( ) scissors
( ) small hammer
( ) screwdriver
( ) pliers
( ) typewriter
( ) typing paper
( ) mikes
( ) lecturn
( ) direction signs
( ) band-aids
( ) music for climate, e.g., tapes, records, etc.

Need
( ) magazines
( ) pointers
( ) clip-boards
( ) tablets
( ) pencils
( ) pencil sharpener
( ) name tags
( ) paper punch
( ) masking tape
( ) transparent tape
( ) rubber bands
( ) ruler
( ) stapler
( ) staple remover
( ) thumb tacks
( ) small nails
( ) copies of Workshop Staff Packet
( ) aspirin
( ) other_____

PARTICIPANT AIDS

Need
( ) pencils
( ) tablets
( ) pencil sharpener
( ) paper clips
( ) notebooks
( ) paper punch
( ) scissors
( ) stapler
( ) clip-boards
( ) lap boards

Need
( ) name tags
( ) place cards
( ) instructions
( ) handouts
( ) water pitchers
( ) glasses
( ) ashtrays
( ) aspirin
( ) band-aids
( ) other_____

NOTE: You may wish to review this list first, checking any items needed for a particular workshop, and then enter them in the aids section of Worksheet Six. If there is insufficient room on Worksheet Six, you may attach this inventory, and enter the Room #/Time information beside the items selected.

REHEARSING

Rehearsing is an activity both simple and crucial. What self-respecting cast would put on a show without a dress rehearsal? The results would be devastating: muffed lines, upstaging, poor timing, dropped props, lost lighting, and terrible reviews. To avoid all those calamaties, rehearse!

What is a good dress rehearsal for a workshop? You guessed it: Refer to the Standard List of Twelve Elements. Needless to say, the rehearsal includes all players if possible. Worksheet 6 is used again for recording rehearsal information. As in the preceeding chapter, instructions are in bold type.

1. Materials

"Obvious!" you say? But how many times have you seen the "show go on" with materials untested. Books should be read, articles reviewed, packages tested, and films watched. If they don't work for the staff, then they don't work.

When you have tried all materials, check the "Rehearsed" blocks.

2. Staff

Each person, using the design (script), plays out his part, or at least the crucial portions of it. He gives his lecture, leads the discussion, demonstrates the model, gives instructions, practices handing-off to next staff performer, etc. Role play is the method here; one person is "it," and the rest play like average participants.

> When each staff member has satisfactorily rehearsed his part as described in the design, check the "Rehearsed" blocks.

3. Consultants

They may balk. Coax them along anyhow. "He who pays the piper . . . ." It may be impossible to do this beforehand, in which case you should make time at the workshop.

> Whenever it is done, check the "Rehearsed" blocks.

4. Participants

"Oh, I can't," you say. I have been known to bounce around the room from chair to chair acting out every sweet/silly/mean potential participant I know anything about. This gives the staff a chance to practice dealing with the different participant styles. And don't feel guilty; the participants are rehearsing (at least in their heads) for you, too.

186

When the staff is prepared to deal with a variety of "characters," check the "Rehearsed" block.

5. Structure

Try out the different structural forms. Check for potential individual/staff/group interactions. Try out the group sizes as planned in the design. If the group is to be a large audience, imagine its size and talk to it.

When you feel comfortable with planned structures, check the "Rehearsed" blocks.

6. Aids

You've got them ready so try them out. If they feel awkward, try them again. If they still feel awkward, get rid of them. If they collapse, fire the stage manager.

For surviving aids, check the "Rehearsed" blocks.

7. Facility

I have worked with staff groups who rehearsed imagined encounters with hotel people. Like how to follow, "What do you *mean*, you've got this room reserved?" Your workshop may depend on it. Since it is an optional activity, however, no blank is provided for your check.

187

8. Accommodations

Go over the Survey and try to predict problems. These can be pretty off beat, e.g., "But I have never slept in a room *alone* before," or "all night, up and down in front of my door, dragging his feet and rattling chains." Again this is optional, so no blank is provided.

9. Food and Refreshments

By all means! Take your sweetie out to dinner.

10. Dates

No special rehearsal needed, unless you've booked a blind date.

11. Travel

You could rehearse the security check, or losing your bags, or just skip it.

12. Promotion

Would you buy it? More important, are *they* buying it? If response is low, you may consider additional or revised promotional efforts.

> **If you choose to make a second contact, now is the time. Record the date in the "2nd Contact Date" blank. When you are satisfied, check appropriate "Rehearsed" blocks.**

13. Time

This is a design check. Do the activities move well?
Are they slow when they should be? Does the coffee
break come off like a flicker film? In effect, you have
now rehearsed the entire design. If changes are indicated, make them on the design worksheet.

PACKING 8

No, you cannot have the secretary do it. Even the most conscientious secretary may not fully appreciate the value of a roll of masking tape, to say nothing of the workshop design, staff packet, or materials, especially if the workshop is to be held in the hinterlands. Have you ever been to a workshop where the leader said, "What we had planned to do was _____"? Sometimes it works out all right; sometimes it doesn't. Why take the risk?

The Standard List of Twelve Elements becomes truer and truer; the Staff Packet Worksheets, your loyal servants. Packing should take place at least one business day before the workshop. This makes it possible to secure missing items. Worksheet 6 instructions are found in bold type.

1. Materials

These are perhaps the most crucial; without them you may have to redesign the entire workshop—on the spot! Find a big clear table and lay out materials in order of use. Check their quality and the number of copies where applicable. When satisfied, place them all in a box (or boxes) marked "Materials." You may want to mark separate boxes "Day 1,"

191

"Day 2," etc. Place nothing else in these boxes. Tape securely. Mark "Do not open before _____."

> Now check the "Packed" blocks on Worksheet 6.

2. Staff

In this case, "packing them" is perhaps too literal. "Sending them packing" has yet another connotation. What you actually do is make certain that they have their notes, staff packets, designs, airplane tickets, etc. Double check departure and arrival times, coordinate dress (if appropriate) and synchronize your watches for the preworkshop team meeting. The rest is in the hands of God and the staff's families.

> When you are relatively satisfied (less anxious) check the "Packed" blocks on Worksheet 6.

3. Consultants

This, of course, depends on finding them. Consultants have the nasty habit of "cutting it close," producing all kinds of ulcerous bile for more regular folks. Consequently, it is a good idea to track them down and have them repeat (to your satisfaction and without the aid of coaching) exactly what they plan to do. If you were rigorously detailed in the written agreement, you may avoid "getting tough" at this point.

> When you are as sure as you can be,
> check the "Packed" blocks on Worksheet
> 6. Be sure to use a pencil.

4. Participants

If a preregistration procedure is involved, count the heads. If participants are in-house, you may want to call a short meeting to reconfirm arrangements. There may still be time to remove obstacles to participant attendance or to unload some of the guaranteed rooms. If the local football team made the playoffs, there may yet be time to reschedule the workshop.

> Do the best you can under the circum-
> stances and check the "Packed" block on
> the worksheet.

5. Structure

The bulk of the checking here must wait for physical proximity to the meeting rooms. If they are in town, you should probably tour them one last time to make certain that they have not shrunk since the survey. However, no block is provided since the crucial check comes in the setting-up phase just before the meeting.

6. Aids

These become increasingly important in direct proportion to the distance from town.

> Check the "Packed" block for each item
> listed on the worksheet as you place it in
> a box.

You may find it handy to organize them by the three categories used earlier, i.e., content aids, staff aids, and participant aids. This will make it easier when setting up. Care should be taken in counting since a tablet shortage can become very frustrating. As a final check, you might again review the "Aids Inventory" to see if your list is actually complete.

7. Facility

Get in touch with the proper facility personnel. Make certain you speak to someone with authority. Reconfirm all arrangements. Be tough if necessary, or someone spending more money may grab your space. Your written agreement (thoroughly detailed) constitutes a contract.

> Check the "Packed" block on the work-
> sheet.

8. Accommodations

Again, you should take the precaution of reconfirming. Many participants arrive early and become very annoyed if a room is not waiting.

> Check the "Packed" block when you are
> certain that there is a room in the inn.

9. Food and Refreshments

Reconfirm all arrangements. **Check the "Packed" blocks.** If the participant check revealed drop-outs, you can save some "bread."

10. Dates

By this time there had best be no question. No block is provided.

11. Travel

Those darned airlines! You know the wisdom of checking this one, particularly when you're traveling on Friday. It's a curious workshop when no staff arrives—very laissez faire.

> **"Packed" blocks have been provided for your convenience.**

12. Promotion

If this has not been previously and continuously checked, you may have packed in vain.

> **If preregistration was involved, attached the "Response" list to Worksheet 6 and check appropriate "Packed" block.**

***   ***   ***

You may now sit back, light up your pipe, or go out to a movie. First, however, make certain you packed your toothbrush.

PART II

Conducting The Workshop

CONDUCTING

Instead of *conducting*, you might also use the words *leading, coordinating, managing,* or *directing.* I mean conducting as in "conducting an orchestra." That is to say that in this role the educator has the responsibility for guiding a diverse number of individuals, grouped according to common interests and thematic developments, through an orchestrated score to a standing ovation. All this with the usual distractions of coughs, closing doors, noisy air vents, shuffling feet and worse.

So far this book has been concerned with a variety of activities that occur prior to the workshop. Attention now shifts to the workshop itself and the adult educator's activities "on stage." While the elements are essentially the same, they are now together, interacting, dynamic, and continuous. Corrrespondingly, the educator's job is more demanding, intense, and exciting. Not only must you continue to be a competent technician, you must also be a skilled leader in a complex human undertaking. If you have planned well, if everything is in a state of expectant readiness, if you are alert yet relaxed, then you may be able to guide the workshop through to a successful conclusion.

This section of the book is devoted to exploring the adult educator's activities in conducting the workshop. As before, the chapters are arranged as nearly as possible in the order that they occur in practice.

Chapter 9: Setting Up—employs the standard elements as a basis for analyzing this preparatory activity.

Chapter 10: Setting the Learning Climate—describes the purpose, ingredients, and behaviors involved in getting the workshop off on the right foot.

Chapter 11: Agreeing on Objectives—explores the methodology and psychology of the educational contract.

Chapter 12: Directing Learning Activities—analyzes the dynamic interaction of elements and the adult educator's role in "harmonizing" them; includes a look at the many-faceted world of group dynamics.

Chapter 13: Closing Shop—details the administrative and janitorial activities that give the workshop that "finished look."

The lights come up on stage. The house is silent. The conductor raises his baton. The workshop is about to begin.

SETTING UP 9

This chapter examines the conductor's activities from the moment he arrives at the meeting facility until he lifts his baton. In this time he must act as drill sergeant, VIP, repairman, and smiling host. Remarks will be primarily concerned with the most complex situation, the dormitory workshop. If yours is the simpler in-house "commuter" workshop, simply scale down the remarks. Be careful, though; those in-house workshops are not as simple as they appear. The tendency to be casual in setting them up can lay your careful planning to waste.

In order to describe this activity, I will utilize the list of twelve elements, plus one. When working with an actual workshop, check your activities against the spaces provided on Worksheet 6 of the Workshop Staff Packet. Again, worksheet instructions are shown in bold type.

1. Materials

Locate the box(es) marked "Materials." Remove the contents carefully, and spread them on a large table. Check them for completeness; count the copies. Arrange them in order of use. If the first session is still some time away (e.g., tomorrow), store materials in a safe place. If the session is about to begin, place materials so that participants will get only the ones you want them to have for the first session. It is a good practice to introduce materials only when you are about to use them in the learning; this avoids needless paper shuffling during the session. If a workshop packet or notebook is provided, participants can insert materials as they are used.

> When you have completed this activity satisfactorily, place a check in the "Set" blocks.

2. Staff

Assemble the staff for a preworkshop briefing. See if each person has a copy of the design, his notes, and any other materials needed for his part of the workshop. Go through the design activity-by-activity and ask each person to describe his role. This includes greeting and registration activities. If the workshop spans more than a day, it is necessary to review only the first day's activities at this time. As a group, consider the need for any special assignments that may have become apparent since arriving. Make those assignments.

> Record them in the blanks provided on Worksheet 6; check the "Set" block by each person's name.

Arrange the time and place of the next team meeting. In longer workshops, it is preferable to meet shortly after the end of the day's activities to debrief, critique, and review the next day's assignments. Worksheet 7, p. 261, is provided for staff notes on each day's activities. It should be passed out at this time.

3. Consultants

If consultants have arrived, include them in the team meeting. If they are scheduled to arrive later, be certain that you have reserved sufficient time to get them properly meshed into the workshop. In some cases your meeting with them may not occur until the workshop is in progress. In any event you should brief them completely with all the data at your disposal, including the climate of the workshop. If you have not done so earlier and dignity permits, rehearse them just as you did your staff and check for notes and materials.

On the worksheet, you may now check the "Rehearsed" and "Set" blocks.

If consultants are going to be around, include them in future team meetings.

4. Participants

Participants should be greeted by a host/hostess as they arrive at the meeting facility and assisted through registration and, if possible, hotel check-in. This is important in setting a good climate. Check to see if staff is doing a friendly job. Participants should be provided with a schedule and an invitation to the social, if one is scheduled. It is also considerate to make available area maps and information on special events, restaurants, etc.

203

At the last possible moment, check to see how many have arrived, enter in appropriate blank on Worksheet 6, and check the "Set" block. Double check to see if you have received any messages concerning delayed arrivals. If so, enter in "Problems" blank.

If yours is an in-house "commuter" workshop, this activity may be meshed into setting the learning climate described in the next chapter. In either case climate-setting is what you are doing for good or ill.

5. Structure

This is one of the major activities at this stage of the game, and you need your VIP manner to properly impress hotel (facility) employees. Explore each meeting room in light of the activities to be held there. Provide hotel staff with a list of tables, chairs, etc., required for each room and the times they are needed. Enter on worksheet.

After carefully examining the room, you may want to prepare sketches of room arrangements. If so, attach to Worksheet 6 and check the "Sketches Attached" spaces. If the hotel is responsible for set-up, give them copies of the sketches. It is judicious to deal not only with manaement, but with the workers as well. By your manner, indicate that tips will be forthcoming for good work.

When all arrangements are complete, check the "Arranged" blocks. The "Set" blocks are reserved for your check just prior to the meeting in that room. By using pencil and eraser, the same blanks will serve for each day's arrangements in a longer workshop.

For more information on possible table and chair arrangements, see the notes and sketches at the end of this chapter.

6. Aids

As with materials, unpack aids and check each item. Try projectors and other mechanical toys. Do you have spare bulbs, parts, etc.?

> **When you feel confident, place a check in the "Set" blocks or reserve these blocks for just before aids are to be used.**

If possible, store aids in rooms where they will be used; otherwise, store them in the team room or your own, if on an economy plan.

> **List times and places they are to be used in the "Room No./Time" spaces on Worksheet 6.**

7. Facility

Double check all arrangements with the hotel (facility); be at your VIP best. Check all equipment that the facility will provide if you did not do so when unpacking aids. Check all services to be provided for participants. Have meeting room problems corrected. Several other items will likely be apparent on the scene.

> **When satisfied, check the "Set" blocks on Worksheet 6.**

8. Accommodations

Make certain that reservations are in order. Arrange to drop rooms for "no-show" participants. If possible assign staff to assist with any room problems.

Check the "Set" block when all are secure within.

9. Food and Refreshments

Review all arrangements for food and refreshments with service personnel and management. Arrange for quick communications in case of unexpected needs.

If you have not already done so, complete the "Room No./Time" spaces on the worksheet and check the "Set" blocks.

10. Dates

There better not be any changes!

11. Travel

Check ground transportation to be used by participants. Sometimes it is possible to make journeys a little smoother. In case of delayed arrivals, special arrangements may be necessary.

"Set" means that there are no strikes and all is well on land and in the air.

206

12. Promotion

You may spice things up with signs, bulletins, news-letters, and party hats, or you may simply envy those fortunate workshops with golden coffers. Directional signs are a must, and advertisements for future workshops are a good idea.

> For any material provided at this point, list on Worksheet 6 and check the appropriate "Set" blocks.

13. Time

Given all the above data, check for implications to the design and make any needed changes there.

*** *** ***

You are now as ready as you will ever be. Take a deep breath. Go have a drink.

ABOUT TABLES AND CHAIRS

This section presents a number of sketches of possible table and chair arrangements. The arrangements are divided into those appropriate for knowledge, skill, and attitude learning. Three sketches for large group arrangements are also provided. Each division includes a discussion of the possible uses of the pictured arrangements, as well as comments concerning the impact of various arrangements on the learning activities. Since comparatively little is known about the effects of the physical environment on learning, feel free to experiment.

Knowledge

For knowledge learning activities, it is often a good idea to use tables. This provides participants with a convenient writing surface. Lap boards or hard-backed notebooks can be substituted, but they may produce a distracting dance as participants attempt to use them while balancing coffee cups and reaching for ashtrays.

There is a much more subtle advantage to using tables in knowledge learning events, they conceal better than half of a participant's body. Freed from the self-consciousness attached to that half, the participant perhaps has additional consciousness to focus on matters of the mind. This is an untested theory, offered for your consideration.

Also untested are a few notions regarding the effects of chairs on knowledge learning. The typical folding chair is uncomfortable and leaves participants feeling insecure. These chairs may assist in knowledge learning when participants are expected to absorb without critiquing or contributing. Armchairs, particularly those of the swivel variety, provide participants a sense of self-contain-ment, and may aid in a knowledge learning situation for which participant contributions are desirable. The extreme case is the wingback or library chair from which participants might pontificate. It is suggested that the physical nature of chairs produces effects quite apart from any status value that may be attributed to particular chairs.

The sketches on the opposite page receive comment below.

Figure 1a: Doubtless familiar, the ubiquitous rectangular table, seating from seven to nine people, serves for all kinds of small group meetings. Table width affects the process level of group interaction; the wider the table, the more formal the interactions tend to be. The "x" at the top of the table represents the educator. This position automatically affords a certain amount of "up-front" control. Consideration should be given the seat at the other end since it, too, has power. Comments by members tend to be directed toward these two positions or to those directly across the table.

Figure 1b: Four tables arranged in a rectangle provide seating for a larger group. The "x's" suggest a panel; the two missing chairs provide a bit of separation. A square arrangement can be produced by rearranging the tables; this reduces the power concentrated at the ends of rectangular arrangements.

Figure 1c: This triangular arrangement produces a more equal distribution of power among members, but it tends to further limit the direction of interactions.

Figure 1d: The two circles of chairs shown in this figure represent the group-on-group structure. The outer group can easily observe the activities of the inner group. This is most appropriate for a knowledge method requiring little writing. Circular shapes fully distribute power and produce the most random pattern of interactions.

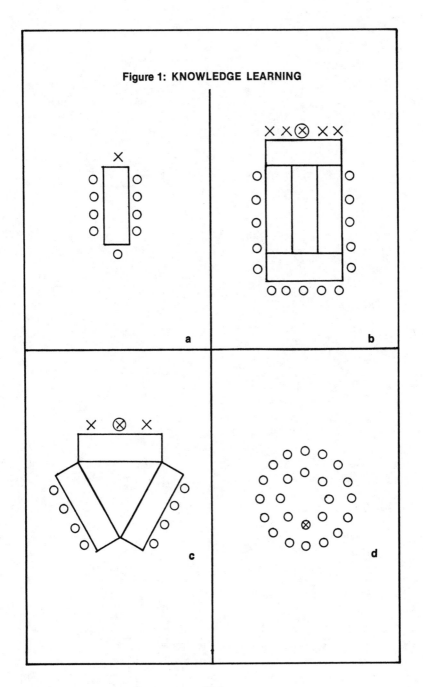

Figure 1: KNOWLEDGE LEARNING

Skill

The main thing required of tables and chairs in skill learning activities is flexibility. The furniture and other props must be made to simulate or approximate the actual situation in which the skill will be used. For example, tables are required for the demonstration and practice of skills that will in real life be practiced at tables. When the application of skills in real life does not involve tables, no tables should be provided. Providing tables for participants who are merely observing can also be a problem, since that makes the participant who is practicing feel even more exposed.

The type of chair used becomes critical only in extreme cases. For example, when participants practice in comfortable armchairs in the workshop, but sit on stools back on the job. When a participant is practicing a "stand up" skill, chairs for observing participants are not unduly disturbing when no tables are provided.

With a little imagination both tables and chairs can be made to symbolize other elements back on the job. This is perfectly adequate for simulating many settings. For certain specialized skills, nothing less than a mockup of the work setting will do. In those cases the work setting itself may be used, provided care is taken that the setting and those in it are not victimized.

Comments regarding the sketches on the opposite page are found below.

Figure 2a: In this figure, the triangular shape is open. This allows the instructor to stand directly in front of practicing participants and participants to gather around the demonstration table. This arrangement is appropriate only for skills that are applied at tables.

Figure 2b: This arrangement allows the instructor to remain seated while demonstrating the skill. It should be used only when the skill being demonstrated can be easily seen by the seated participants. As in the open triangle, this arrangement allows the instructor to stand directly in front of practicing participants.

Figure 2c: This is a sketch picturing the fish-bowl structure. It is appropriate for the practice of skills that do not involve tables. The two figures in the center represent two participants facing each other in a role-play situation. All others are observers. As you can see, instructor power is reduced by the instructor randomly selecting a chair in the circle.

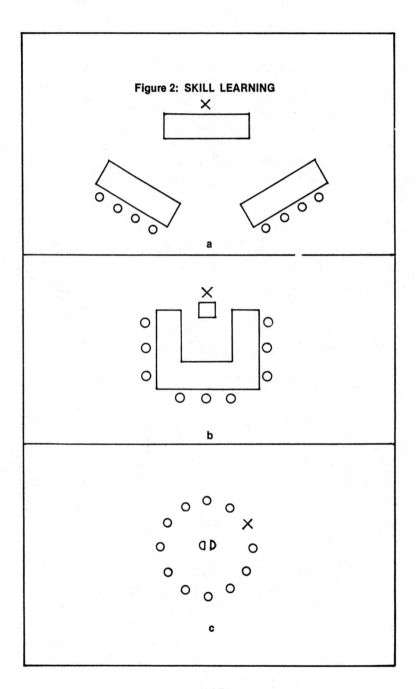

Figure 2: SKILL LEARNING

a

b

c

215

Attitude

Tables are a definite hindrance when attitude learning is attempted. The body concealment described earlier as an advantage in knowledge learning becomes a cover-up in attitude learning. Tables can become a shield against the impact of attitude stimuli. Attitude change may be more difficult for participants seated behind tables.

Chairs may also be a problem. Wingback and library chairs offer a good place to hide; swivel armchairs can serve as a defensive weapon. The discomfort and insecurity of typical folding chairs may be an advantage in attitude learning. Better still is seating participants on the floor on cushions or on the carpet. This, however, may run headlong into cultural or personal values different from the ones to be learned, and as a result, cancel the beneficial effects of getting away from chairs.

Following are comments regarding the three figures on page 219.

Figure 3a: In attitude learning, circular arrangements are preferable since the power positions inherent in other arrangements can be destructive. The instructor should neutralize his power by taking a seat in the group as a participant. He should also act like any other participant.

Figure 3b: This "shotgun" arrangement is accomplished by simply scattering the chairs. Personal space is very important to people in attitude-change situations. Scattered chairs allow participants to provide themselves with a certain amount of safety by establishing their own personal space and distance from others. Be prepared for the tendency of participants to arrange the chairs in some regular pattern such as rows, and decide beforehand if this is to be allowed. If not, an understanding comment regarding the safety found in

217

rows may be a way of starting a discussion of attitudes and their effects. You should also guard against the tendency of some participants to attempt to force others into a particular arrangement. In attitude learning, force can be very threatening. The goal of this arrangement is the reduction of threat.

Figure 3c: This sketch represents the extreme in attitude learning and is not recommended for most situations. If used, a practitioner skilled in human psychology is a must. The outer circle represents some immovable element such as a wall or circular screens. One means of escaping when things get heavy in group activity is moving back or leaning back out of the group perimeter. In the pictured arrangement the line of escape is cut off since the only way to lean back far enough to be out of the fire is to move further into the group. As pictured here, the instructor controls the exit. This example is provided primarily to illustrate the impact of the environment on human learning.

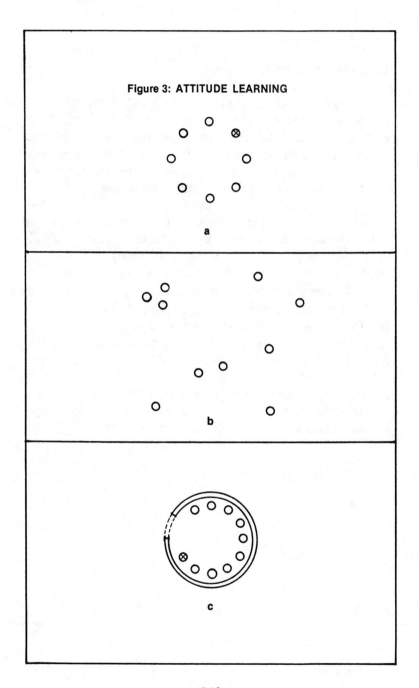

Figure 3: ATTITUDE LEARNING

a

b

c

Large Group Arrangements

Large groups are not often good structures for learning purposes. Their effectiveness is limited to knowledge learning that requires limited participant contribution and interchange. On the opposite page, only semicircular arrangements are shown since straight rows are not conducive to adult learning activities.

Figure 4a: This sketch pictures the familiar semicircular row arrangement. The center aisle provides easier access. Care should be taken to provide enough space for people to walk without stepping on toes. At least a little space between chairs is also desirable.

Figure 4b: This semicircular arrangement adds tables for writing convenience. It also makes subgrouping for discussion or "buzz" purposes easy.

Figure 4c: This semicircular arrangement adds to a pleasant climate when round tables are available. When tables are not available, chairs can still be arranged in this manner to provide subgroup ease and to remove that "isolated in an audience" feeling. As pictured, the angle of the chairs allows a direct unencumbered view of the stage.

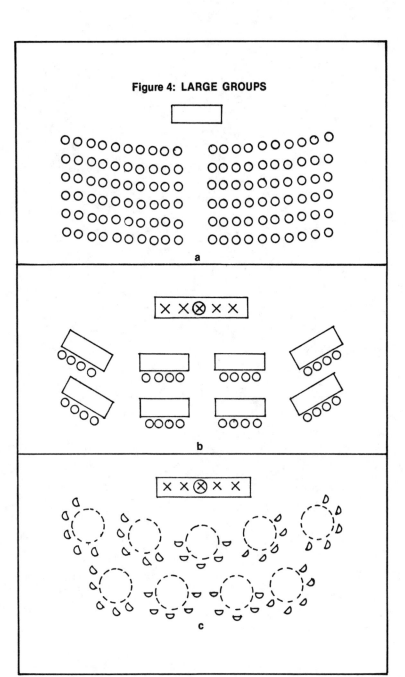

Figure 4: LARGE GROUPS

SETTING THE LEARNING CLIMATE

The first few minutes of the workshop are the most crucial. If they are interesting, relevant, and pleasant, problems which may arise later can be resolved with a minimum of loss to the learning. If the first minutes are boring, pointless, and unpleasant, the most precious gems of learning are likely to be lost in the mud of misunderstanding, incomprehension, or apathy. If you cannot always produce a positive attitude toward learning, you should at least attempt to insure that you are not the cause of a negative one. Paraphrasing Mager, the learning climate should be arranged in such a way that the participant is in the presence of as many pleasant conditions as possible and as few as possible unpleasant ones.

This is a tall order, but if you did your planning well and if you planned an environment for adults, you have already taken a giant step in setting a pleasant learning climate. Further, if you chose the democratic approach to needs assessment, there is a good chance that the climate is already blessed with a positive participant attitude and a benevolent word from management.

What remains? Let's take it step by step.

1. Greeting Participants

Adults seem to respond better to a handshake than a cold stare meaning "take your seat." They like the sound of their names better than "you there" or "you people." They are accustomed to addressing leaders in terms other than "Herr Professor" or "Sarg." They are often less forward than children in sidling-up to say "hi" to the new adult. Introductions are in order all around. Name tags or place cards may also be useful in keeping salutations personal.

If everyone is already acquainted, then a few minutes spent discussing the weather (contrary to common wisdom) can work wonders for the climate.

2. Getting Everyone Comfortable

Adults respond better to the warm offer of strong coffee than to the warm/cold introduction of a strong/weak speaker. They usually prefer to find their own seats rather than having seats assigned. The announcement of coming breaks and restroom locations is a load off everyone's mind. Invitations to move chairs or change them, sit on the floor, and remove shoes, coats, and ties adds the comfort of home. Music soothes ragged nerves.

3. Spelling out the Ground Rules

Adults (unlike most children) are very interested in knowing the rules of the game. In this case, "spelling them out" amounts to describing in general terms the ways in which participants and resources may relate during the learning experience. In the democratic approach, it might go something like this:

> "These resources (people, materials) are here for you. Feel free to use them, call for more, whatever. Stop me (us) if you don't understand something; suggest that we move on if you already understand it."

4. Warming up

In Chapter Four I described the structure of warm-ups more fully. Here, I will address their usage. Adults are people who are overworked and underslept. Adults are people who have pressing concerns beyond the learning experience. Adults are people whose minds are wont to wander to those concerns. Warm-ups help adults wake up. They lighten the burden of concerns. If related to the content, warm-ups produce a climate of "readiness."

5. Discussing Expectations

By this I mean a general preview of what is to come followed by a discussion of its relevance. This leads naturally to the next activity in the workshop, agreeing on objectives. If for some reason expectations don't match the previewed activities, the time to start discussing changes is now, before you plow into a recitation of preset objectives. Adults are people who respond better to objectives (self-set or not) if the objectives meet their expectations. Expectations can change. Adults are people who respond better to objectives that they know they can change (at least a little). Besides, objectives that are open to change are changed less often and more often achieved.

***   ***   ***

These are the major steps; you may think of others. There is nothing magic in the order; I often switch numbers three and four and sometimes add a discussion of expectations to the introductions. It may appear that the above process is time consuming, and it should be if participants are strangers or if the workshop extends over a number of days. For short workshops (one day or less), climate setting can be done fully in as few as fifteen minutes.

STYLE VARIATIONS

Extreme Authoritarian—Not interested in names, comfort, warmth, or expectations. Holds participants accountable for unstated rules, such as proper comportment, promptness, and respect for authority.

Extreme Laissez Faire—Often the entire workshop is taken up with climate setting. While this may be humanly rewarding, it can be frustrating for the serious learner.

Moderate Authoritarian—"Glad hands" it a bit. Provides coffee for the purpose of looking good rather than from concern for the effect of the climate on learning.

Moderate Laissez Faire—May come off a little ingrati-
atingly in concern for human needs. Consequently
may find it difficult to push on into learning activities.

Democratic—The good-natured directness detailed in the
text.

AGREEING ON OBJECTIVES

11

This is the second most crucial activity in conducting the workshop. It serves little purpose to specify objectives if you keep them secret. Secret objectives would help *you* know if paticipants had learned (likely they have not), but they would not help the participants know what they were supposed to learn; and they would not help keep everyone moving in the direction of the learning. Perhaps the main reason for specifying objectives is that they may serve as a beacon for "voyaging" learners. And who knows, out in the open like that they might even be of help in keeping you on course.

It is only slightly better to state objectives without gaining agreement. Participants would then know where they were *supposed* to go, but information without commitment has gotten many leaders shot in the back, or more typically it has sent them charging enthusiastically up the hill—alone. "Agreement" is actually too loose a word; what you want is a contract. Since a contract is a document that specifies as completely as possible the minimum performance expected of each and every party thereto, the GLO's and SLO's described earlier in this book constitute a good draft, ready for final revision and signing.

Most of us are not accustomed to such a formalized procedure in learning situations, and as a result, contracting on learning objectives may sound too much like a business deal. We have been led to believe that learning is a mystical, sacred activity, hardly susceptible to the hard-nosed tactics of the business world. Curiously, that is the same kind of line put out by the "helluva-deal" hustler in business. In both cases it is likely to mean that the deal looks a little shaky in broad daylight.

Another example is seen with the repairman who refuses to state an estimate on the seemingly reasonable grounds that "he will have to get into it and see." Once he's got it all torn apart, he gives you the bad word, and since you have no other choice, he fixes it and presents you with a staggering bill. A week later it doesn't work.

Somewhere in between is the handshake partnership in which both partners end up feeling taken advantage of when the venture fails.

Workshops without a contract tend to lead to one or more of the following results:

1. Activities proceed; participants do not learn.

2. Activities proceed; participants fade away.

3. Activities proceed; participants endure and (untested) say good things at the end but demonstrate no changed behavior back on the job.

4. Activities proceed; participants demonstrate the new behavior in

the workshop and refuse to use it
back on the job.

5. Activities proceed; participants discover that the educator is just doing his job with no clear idea of the
   outcome.

6. Activities proceed and by some
   magic hit target; participants
   learn and go back to the job and
   use their new competency.

There is a one-in-six chance of success. The chances are
considerably better when everyone contracts on the intended outcomes.

A final objection might be that such specific contracting is offensive to adult sensitivities. And it is, if
adults are given no opportunity to shape the objectives,
are forced to agree by some coercion, such as a paycheck.
Given a free bargaining opportunity, however, clear,
honored agreements between people are among the most
adult of human interactions. Adults are much more likely
to do something they've agreed to than to do something you think they should.

THE PROCESS

Let's take a look at how this agreement might be
achieved.

1. Reviewing Needs

A review of needs follows immediately after the discussion of expectations described in "Setting the

Learning Climate." Presumably these needs were selected by one of the two methods described in Chapter 1. As such they are well supported by reality. If the democratic approach was used, the needs also have the advantage of being agreed upon by the participants. A democratic needs assessment followed by a discussion of expectations allows participants to refresh their memories. Reviewing the needs agreed upon should then serve as a reinforcement unless needs have changed. If there have been changes, differences should now be dealt with and needs added or deleted.

2. Exploring Objectives

Since specifying objectives is a fairly precise, technical activity, quite often the objectives have been written by the adult educator back at his desk. He must now see if participants accept them as accurate translations of their needs. A good way to do this is to break the group into subgroups of three (triads) for the purpose of a detailed exploration of the objectives (either one per triad or each triad considering all objectives). After triads have taken a few minutes to consider the objective and the means of evaluation, each is given an opportunity to critique the objective and the realism of its test.

If some needs were deleted, the groups should explore only the objectives relating to the remaining needs. If needs were added, new objectives may be formulated and learning activities added for them. If this is not feasible, agree with participants to take them up at a later time.

232

3. Modifying Objectives

With the assistance of the reporting triads, you now attempt to make modificiations to the objectives that will be at least somewhat acceptable to all participants. If you are not flexible enough to do this, contracting is a hoax and worse than no agreement at all. The old song of "Give it a try. You'll understand as you get into it," is transparent.

4. Contracting

Modified objectives in hand, you are now ready to "close the deal." This may take the form of an affirmative show of hands or a "speak now or hold your peace." However you do it, it should be very clear that a contract has been made.

Agreeing on objectives can be a time consuming process if many objectives are involved. In such case, it may be prudent and more comprehensible to consider only the objectives for a particular day's activities. Take up the others as you get to them. Sufficient contracting time should be planned into the design. Too little time set aside for contracting is a common error of beginning designers.

STYLE VARIATIONS

Extreme Authoritarian and Extreme Laissez Faire—No objectives, and no agreement.

Moderate Authoritarian—Attempts to motivate participants to accept precisely written objectives.

233

Moderate Laissez Faire—Sensitive, warm, *general* agreement on *general* directions for learning. Works fine so long as there are no hidden minimums.

Democratic—As always with democratic efforts, the very time consuming process described above.

DIRECTING LEARNING ACTIVITIES 12

This is where the modern adult educator shines. He is like a field general under fire, with all necessary resources, equipment, and personnel at his command; with total authority for his decisions and sufficient knowledge and confidence to make them; with a vareity of strategies and the skill and boldness to execute them; and with a reservoir of personal behavior that ranges from command to comradeship and the wisdom to choose the behavior appropriate to the situation. Educators in traditional settings seldom enter learning engagements with such a sense of adventure.

Let's see how the educator might act in commanding the various elements.

1. Materials

By this time, the educator has demonstrated his adroitness in organizing details. In the midst of learning, he regards his materials with healthy skepticism. If they are not meeting needs, he is quick to change them, adapt them, reorganize them, or get new ones. His flexibility in making changes includes both appropriate seriousness and humor.

2. Staff

He has, of course, picked the best. He is the leader. He takes staff needs seriously. He listens to staff problems and suggestions. He schedules timely team meetings. He shares information, ideas, and feelings. He coordinates staff activities and reorganizes when needed. He provides constructive criticism offstage; he supports staff onstage by his attitude and a limited amount of discrete coaching. He accepts criticism and invites coaching from staff. He inspires the staff in meeting the needs of participants.

3. Consultants

The modern adult educator is dedicated to the learning, not to the consultants. As such, he leads consultants just as if they were staff.

4. Participants

In his relations with participants, the adult educator is many things. Below you will find a few of them gleaned from a variety of experiences. If some seem contradictory, they are made consistent by their adherence to the learning. None of us can do all of these things, but we can try to learn new ones as we increase our skill.

> He listens carefully and accurately.

> He can recall events, interactions, and conversations accurately.

> He is supportive of participant efforts.

236

He encourages participants to try new behaviors.

He does not impose his own values or opinions.

He respects feelings and is free to express his own.

He is patient.

He is responsive and undefensive when criticized.

He can demonstrate genuine anger when appropriate.

He serves as chief recorder.

He normally directs activities with quiet authority.

He directs activities with stern commands when that will move the learning past frustration.

He is trusting.

He is interested in the content.

He provides useful and timely feedback on performance.

He is nonjudgmental.

He stimulates interest and suggests new possibilities.

He is capable of true dialogue.

He reinforces learning.

He models desirable attitudes and behaviors.

He counsels with individual participants.

He is capable of showing a wide range of
genuine human emotion.

He is flexible, open to change.

He is consistent in word and deed.

He is a diplomat.

He assures that his staff behaves appropriately in the above ways.

In addition, in longer workshops it is always useful
to have some staff person on duty to assist with
individual problems.

5. Structures

In the design phase, the modern adult educator
demonstrated foresight in the selection of appropriate structures. Nonetheless, he is constantly observant of weaknesses. He is sensitive to interactions
among participants, group, and staff. He allows
individual changes. He helps resolve conflicts. In
adversity, he blends humor with seriousness.

6. Aids

The educator is adroit in manipulating the tools of
the trade. When they don't work, he fixes them, has
them fixed, or throws them out of the room. He is
constantly checking to see if participants have tablets and sharpened pencils.

7. Facilities

Aware of the environment and its impact on learning, the educator constantly rearranges and tries new combinations. He attempts to regulate the temperature. He negotiates with hotel (facility) people; he is commanding when necessary. He is flexible and finds a new way if he loses.

8. Accommodations

The adult educator is sympathetic and does what he can to keep lodgings from interfering with the learning.

9. Food and Refreshments

Since an educator also eats and drinks, he is aware of the needs of others. He is quick to resupply the coffee. He explores the neighborhood for new culinary delights.

10. Dates

The alert educator keeps an eye on the calendar; if events are running over, he makes arrangements early. He assists participants with late checkouts. He is quick to schedule tentative future dates when new needs arise; he does not leave needs dangling.

11. Travel

The educator assigns staff to assist participants with return arrangements. When daily transportation to the workshop becomes a problem, he works with participants to improve arrangements.

12. Promotion

His behavior in the workshop promotes future workshops.

13. Time

The educator is constantly aware of pacing; he speeds up or slows down as appropriate to the learning. The clock is not his boss. He lengthens activities or shortens them as a result of deliberations with participants. The agenda is a servant.

14. Methods

Aware that the best planned methods will sometimes not work, the adult educator is ready to change them, try others. He enjoys the possibility of creating new ones on the spot. He is skilled in directing many of them.

15. Energy/Attention

The educator's attention never wavers (ahem!), but he is tolerant of human frailties. He is sensitive to fidgeting and crossed legs, and he adds breaks when needed. He notices slumped bodies and glazed eyes and adds warm-ups when appropriate.

16. Climate

An adult educator balances and harmonizes all the above elements to constantly provide a climate supportive of learning. He carries the climate with

him in his own behavior and steers staff in avoiding
storms.

STYLE VARIATIONS

Extreme Authoritarian—Full steam ahead and damn the
torpedoes.

Extreme Laissez Faire—Too open to exert leadership;
everyone for himself.

Moderate Authoritarian—Tends to display the enthusiasm and encouragement of a super-salesman.

Moderate Laissez Faire—May be annoyingly helpful; pli-
able rather than flexible. This may be effective when
the participants are very adult.

Democratic—The good old boys; like the field general
described above, employs a range of behaviors depending on the needs of the learning situation.

SUMMARY

The challenge is obvious. Does it sound impossible?
It isn't. A reasonably sensitive and confident beginner
can do an acceptable job his first time out, provided he is
truthful and undefensive. There is always room for
growth. It can be fun. If you choose it as a career or an
avocation, you may wish to attend workshops devoted to
practicing behaviors needed in directing learning activities.

***   ***   ***

What Follows in This Chapter

"Working with Group Dynamics"—a very practical exploration of the wonderland of groups, complete with helpful tips.

"Worksheet 7"—a worksheet that provides a format for staff observations on each day's activities.

WORKING WITH GROUP DYNAMICS

The adult educator's interest in group dynamics is neither primarily scientific nor even scholarly. Adult educators are interested in group dynamics because they do most of their work in groups. Practitioners need to know when a group is cold, when it is eager, and when it is hostile. They need to know when the group is blocking an individual's learning and when an individual is blocking the learning of others in the group. Most important, they need to know what to *do* about it!

With this in mind, I will hold the theory to a minimum, and add helpful tips wherever possible.

DEFINITIONS

In this section, I am speaking of relatively small groups with a membership range of between three to fifty members. Groups with a larger number of members (e.g. assemblies, audiences, organizations) have dynamics of their own. However these larger bodies are often composed of smaller groups and are consequently subject to some of the following comments.

In *Introduction to Group Dynamics*, Malcolm Knowles defines a group as having the following general qualities:

1) **A definable membership**—a collection of two or more people identifiable by name or type.

2) **Group consciousness**—the members think of themselves as a group, have a "collective perception of unity," a conscious identification with each other.

3) **A sense of shared purpose**—the members have the same "object model" or goals or ideals.

4) **Interdependence in satisfaction of needs**—the members need the help of one another to accomplish the purpose for which they joined the group.

5) **Interaction**—the members communicate with one another, influence one another, react to one another.

6) **Ability to act in a unitary manner**— the group can behave as a single organism.[4]

Sound like "Mission Impossible?" Well, clearly this refers to an ideal group, a group that has been together long enough to work out some of the kinks. More clearly, this does not describe the groups that adult educators often encounter, such as audiences, involuntary assemblages, individualists, lost sheep, and mobs.

Now you know what to work for. Here is how you get it.

INSIDE GROUPS

In your role as director of learning activities, you are often outside the group, and all too often you serve as an excuse for participants to sit there and do nothing. Here are some ingredients you might consider in helping groups work.

Group Norms

There is a great deal of theoretical material about group norms. What the practitioner needs, however, is a good working model of group norms which may be used to assess their effects on all kinds of groups. The family unit is perhaps the clearest model since most of us have a great deal of experience in responding to the group norms found there. Additionally, family norms are usually more "out front" and easier to spot. You are invited to consider the norms of families with which you have experience while reading the following comments.

Essentially, group norms are composed of permissions and restrictions. They give group members permission to behave in certain ways, and they prevent them from behaving in other ways. All groups have norms; some are more binding than others. Some groups have norms that are better established than those of other groups. Depending on the membership, even newly formed groups may have strongly established norms. New members entering an established group must adapt to the established permissions and restrictions of the group; their entrance into the group may begin to change the norms.

Group norms may concern themselves with anything under the sun. There may be permission to think and a restriction on action. Members may or may not be expected to smile. "Speaking one's mind" may be out of the question; off-color jokes may be encouraged. Competition may be in, cooperation out. Group norms affect everything that happens inside groups. Keep them in mind while considering the remaining ingredients of group dynamics.

245

Levels of Group Functioning

Have you ever been in a group of people and noticed that your mouth was talking and your head nodding all by themselves, while your nerves were picking up the underground messages of the scene? Good. You are well on your way to being a successful workshop leader.

That underground action is referred to as the group's **process**. It is made up of interpersonal relationships, feelings, attitudes, looks, postures, gestures, and intonations. In describing the process, you might tell how a group deals with conflict or how it gets itself back on track. In short, process is the medium of group work. The work itself is referred to as the **content**, i.e., the ideas, motions, proposals, opinions, decisions, and so on that the group is focusing around.

Functional Roles

Like most other things, groups work by dividing labor among their members. Often without discussion, several functional roles will occur naturally in groups. In healthy groups actual functional tasks are constantly shared by the members, even though roles may be formally designated and members selected to fill them. Here are the most common roles:

leader/chairperson
recorder/secretary
reporter/spokesperson
observer/parliamentarian
contributor/member

Leadership Styles

In this context, "leadership" refers to the focal point of a group's energies at any given time. It does not necessarily correspond to any of the functional roles just listed. The three styles I have relied on in this book come from group dynamics theory. Once again, they are:

1) Autocratic (authoritarian)

2) Laissez Faire

3) Democratic

And again, each has its place in this world. In healthy groups, the leadership style varies with the situation.

Behavior of Members

According to the theorists, group members demonstrate three different types of behaviors:

1) Task-directed behaviors—those behaviors which move a group along toward its task.

2) Maintenance behaviors—those behaviors which lubricate communication and salve wounds.

3) Self-centered behaviors—those behaviors which satisfy themselves regardless of, or in spite of, group needs. Otherwise known as ego trips.

The first type of behavior is associated with the content level in groups; the other two with the process level.

Clearly, a successful director of adult learning activities must know how to get the most out of task-directed and maintenance behaviors and what to do about the self-centered type. Let's take a closer look.

Task-Directed Behaviors

Initiating/contributing	Offering new ideas, new ways of seeing the problem; suggesting solutions for difficulties the group has encountered, new ways of organizing. (**Tip:** You must often do this yourself, but you should be on a sharp lookout for a group member to replace you.
Information seeking/giving	Asking for or giving clarification in terms of facts, factual adequacy, or authoritative information. (**Tip:** This one comes easy; directors can relax.)
Opinion seeking/ giving	Asking for or giving an opinion of values pertinent to the group's task. (**Tip:** This one abounds; cherish it—up to a point!)

248

Elaborating	Expounding on another's idea or suggestion. (**Tip:** When you see this one, nurture it! Too often, no one listens to what anyone else is saying.)
Coordinating	Pulling ideas together, showing relationships, coordinating activities of group members. (**Tip:** When someone takes this job away from you, it shows what a good director you are!)
Orienting	Telling "where it's at," calling it back where it "oughta be." (**Tip:** The better your session, the more this is needed. If you have managed to get yourself into the group this is a good way for you to behave, but don't be stingy if someone else wants a go at it.)
Evaluating	Subjecting the work of the group to some standard or set of standards. (**Tip:** If the tone is not too harsh or sarcastic, great! Let it run.)
Moving/shaking	Prodding the group on to action, decision, or a higher calling. (**Tip:** You may miss some interesting stories because of this, but usually it is good for the group's learning. Don't stand in the way.)

Recording	Writing suggestions, decisions. (**Tip:** Be sure that men take a hand at this, too!)

Maintenance Behaviors

Encouraging	Praising, agreeing with, and accepting the contributions of others. (**Tip:** Encourage it.)
Harmonizing	Mediating differences and reconciling disagreements between other members, relieving tensions with humor. (**Tip:** You must use your judgement on this one. It is often good, but sometimes things need to get out in the open rather than covered up.)
Compromising	Members meeting half way in order to move the group. (**Tip:** You certainly would look foolish trying to stop it.)
Gatekeeping	Keeping lines of communication open by encouragement or by directing traffic. (**Tip:** A good behavior for educators and other humanitarians.)
Process observing	Commenting on group process when useful. (**Tip:** Practice it!)

Following	Going along with movement of group, serving as an audience for those who have ideas. (**Tip:** Every group has followers. Silence does not necessarily mean a lack of participation. Be sure before you pinch a participant.)

Self-Centered Behaviors

Aggression	Putting others down, sarcastic humor, taking credit for someone else's idea. (**Tip:** If someone in the group does not put a stop to it, you must. Do it as gently as possible, but do it!)
Blocking	Being negative, stubborn, and resistant, blocking movement. (**Tip:** If it happens in the early stages of the learning process, focus the group away from it. Later, if you've done your job, the group's momentum should take care of it.)
Recognition seeking	Just what it says. (**Tip:** This is usually harmless, though pathetic and embarrassing. Be kind.)
Playing	Horseplay, nonchalance, side conversations, reading the paper. (**Tip:** Some good, some bad, but don't let it go too far.)

251

Dominating	Interrupting, talking all the time, manipulating. (**Tip:** You might give him a project, send him on an errand, or add a strong new person to the group. However you do it, get him off-stage!)
Shoulder crying	Constantly telling troubles, insecurities, fears. (**Tip:** Can become a real drag, but let the group deal with it.)
Special interest pleading	Speaking forever in behalf of some cause, i.e., kindness to animals, rights for minorities, participation of the "grass roots." (**Tip:** If it's off the subject and blocking the rest of the group, you may have to stop it. Try countering with a balancing special interest, or consider alternatives described for dominating behavior. Be aware of your own prejudices.)

NOTE: The above listing of behaviors does not attempt to be complete. Please feel free to use your own eyes and ideas.

Complex Behaviors

Fortunately no one person behaves the same way all the time. Real people shift behaviors to fit situations and groups they are in. In addition, real people quite often play out two or more behaviors at once.

Here are three complex behaviors which I have found troublesome. Encountering participants directly by bringing these behaviors "out front" borders on therapy, it may also have economic repercussions on your workshop from disgruntled participants. These are but three of many possible combinations.

Elaborating/ dominating

Elaborating on any and every idea in such a fluid fashion that the group does not notice the manipulative distortions of the original ideas. (**Tip:** Stop everything, take over the stage, and reorient the group.)

Encouraging/ dominating

Praising and encouraging the ideas of others in order to control them. It may be so flattering that no one wants to stop it. (**Tip:** You might try a little honest critique, but you may make everyone mad by doing so.)

Dominating/shoulder crying/aggression

Assertive sympathy seeking accompanied with and followed by hostility. This is similar to the game identified by transactional

analysis called "Yes, but . . ."
(**Tip:** I had trouble with this
combination. Above all, don't
play into it by trying to be helpful. You may have to break up
the group and change to individual learning activities.)

Group Decision-Making Models

This is merely to suggest some of the ways that
decisions are made in groups. Some of them you know,
some of them you know but haven't thought about,
some of them may be new. You may want to encourage
some of these decision-making methods and even build
them into your design; others would be better
discouraged.

Inaction

Someone makes a suggestion,
and it is rejected by being
ignored.

Self-authorization

Someone suggests that the
group take a certain action, then
proceeds to take it without
waiting for reaction.

Cliques

Subgroups strategize either
before the meeting or through
signals and intuition in the
meeting to make decisions for
the entire group.

Pressure

As in "No one disagrees, do
they?"

Assumption	As in "I believe we are all in accord."
Majority rule	The greatest good for the greatest number. Timing of votes often becomes important, since the greatest number has a way of shifting.
Unanimity	When the vibes clearly indicate that everyone is for it, often without votes or discussion.
Straw votes	Tentative or initial indicators of potential agreement or disagreement; narrow the range or debate.
An agreed upon procedure	Such as in stating problems, supporting with data, suggesting alternative solutions, reality testing. In effect, all agree to go with the decision indicated by the process and the data.
Consensus	Involves an exploration of ideas, with care being taken not to reach conclusions too quickly. Requires that each and every member agree at least partially to a decision. Can be very effective, but runs the danger of "group-think," an evil we have seen something of lately.

Jamming

This is my own contribution; it takes its name from jazz. In it, a theme is struck (a concern, a problem, an opportunity, a lark). Someone has an idea and takes off with it (solos). No one interrupts. When he finishes, there is a short pause for reflection (this also aids good listening habits).

The next person does *not* make a counterpoint, or an elaboration, or any kind of reaction to the first player's solo; rather he gets into his own solo. Again, a pause follows (should be at least one minute long).

Without reaction, the next person does his solo. And so on. It is recognized that no contribution is too plain or too far out; all have value.

After some time and a number of sets, a player suddenly combines one member's plain idea with another member's crazy one, and everyone knows simultaneously that "this is it," a decision often much better than that possible by any other process.

OUTSIDE GROUPS

Now that we have dissected the insides of groups and you know what to do in there, let's see them from the outside as a whole. Observe their surfaces. Look at them. How do they feel? What should you do about it?

Cold groups	They are just like your old car in the morning. You've got to warm them up, give 'em the gas. Make certain your planned warm-up activities are sufficiently active.
Hostile groups	You either have to know or find out why they are hostile. If they are hostile at the beginning of a session, something is forced; they have not "bought in." Call attention to it. See if you can get it right. Be flexible. If hostility appears later in the session, there may be frustration or confusion. You may need to push the learning on through to a clearing.
Sleepy groups	Too much lecture, not enough active participation. Get them moving. Often happens right after lunch. Plan something active.
Off-the-subject groups	Maybe the subject was not the right one. Ask.
Dense groups	No matter how clearly you state the task or how often you repeat it, they just won't understand. This usually amounts to task avoidance. Either the trust level is too low, the task is difficult enough to be threatening, or

257

they simply do not feel prepared. Bring it out in the open. Find out. Refer to the objective and see if it is still agreeable.

Pass-the-buck groups   The group implies that you have done something wrong or have not done something you should have. This is often passive/aggressive behavior. They get you to pick up the ball, then **WHAMMO!** On the other hand, they may be right. But if it really is the group's job, don't pick it up.

Fun and games groups   Everything is just so much fun there's hardly any time left over for work. Shout "Remember the Objective"; if that fails, simply join in and forget it.

There are others, but you get the idea.

BETWEEN GROUPS

When two or more groups are bumping around on the same turf, there are a limited number of possible outcomes between them.

1. They may not notice each other, but it's unlikely.

258

2. They may notice each other and simply coexist.

3. All but one may leave.

4. They may merge.

5. They may compete, sometimes until all but one group is eliminated.

6. When there are more than two groups, the place is rife with endless possibilities for intrigues and and collaboration.

7. They may cooperate.

As a practitioner of adult education, you need to remember that groups form identities and "territories." If you start competitive activities for a little fun, you may need to follow with cooperative ones or perhaps change the composition of the groups. Unbridled competition can wreck your workshop.

***** ***** *****

Worksheet 7 is found on the following page. It may be used by staff for recording observations on each day of workshop activity. If you choose, it may be completed by selected participants. It is designed to be largely self-instructing. Anyone completing it should be encouraged to describe problems and suggestions in his own words. It is not necessary that he read the text. This worksheet should be given to each staff member at the first team meeting of the workshop. They may record their assignments for the first day's activities on this form, and as the day progresses, jot down notes regarding the activities. This provides good data for the team meeting at the end of the day.

Given the complexity of data on Worksheet 6 and the need for maintaining centralized control of any data changes, it may be advisable for the workshop director to maintain the *only* copy of that worksheet and provide other staff with Worksheet 7 for their suggested changes.

STAFF ASSIGNMENTS AND OBSERVATIONS

Workshop

Name   Date

---

1. MATERIALS

1) Are the materials meeting workshop needs?

2) Suggested improvements

3) Assignments

---

2. STAFF

1) Is staff working well together?

2) Suggested improvements

3) Assignments

---

3. CONSULTANTS

1) Are consultants adding to learning?

2) Are they working well with staff?

3) Suggested improvements

4) Assignments

---

4. PARTICIPANTS

1) How well is staff relating to participant needs (real or imagined)?

2) Suggested improvements

3) Assignments

---

5. STRUCTURE

1) How well are structures supporting learning?

2) Suggested improvements

3) Assignments

---

6. AIDS

1) Problems

2) Suggested improvements

3) Assignments

---

7. FACILITY

1) Problems

2) Suggested improvements

3) Assignments

---

8. ACCOMMODATIONS

1) Problems

2) Suggested improvements

3) Assignments

---

9. FOOD AND REFRESHMENTS

1) Problems

2) Suggested improvements

3) Assignments

---

10. DATES

1) Will closing time need to be changed?

2) Additional dates

3) Assignments

---

11. TRAVEL

1) Problems in getting to or from workshop

2) Suggested improvements

3) Assignments

---

12. PROMOTION

1) Opportunities for further workshops

2) Suggested topics

3) Assignments

261

13. TIME

1) Is pace appropriate?
2) Suggested improvements
3) Assignments

14. METHODS

1) Which two methods worked best?
2) Which methods encountered problems?
3) Which remaining methods need to be changed?
4) Assignments

15. ENERGY/ATTENTION

1) Are more/less breaks needed?
2) Are more/less warmup activities needed?
3) Suggested improvements
4) Assignments

16. CLIMATE

1) What is the climate of the session(s)?
2) Is it supportive of learning?
3) Suggested improvements
4) Assignments

II. GROUP OBSERVATIONS

Use the following guide to help identify group or individual problems that may be blocking learning. Add any other which might apply.

1. Group norm problems, resulting from group permissions and restrictions

2. Group functioning problems resulting from process/content imbalance

3. Functional role problems resulting from disfunctional division of labor

4. Leadership style problems

5. Problems resulting from individual behavior

6. Problems in group decision-making

7. Problems in competition/cooperation between groups

8. Others

262

CLOSING SHOP 13

You have come this far. A few more minutes won't hurt and may save money, law suits and other inconvenience. Since by this time your Staff Packet is probably all shot to hell and your eyes are somewhere beyond bloodshot, there is a fresh, simple, very readable worksheet for this activity. (Worksheet 8.)

1. Materials

Pack up the remnants. Note any missing items on the worksheet. Conduct a frantic search for any missing films.

2. Staff

You can suffer through the final debriefing and critique now or later at home. If everyone is going off immediately on a vacation, now is the time since no one will care a week from now. Bonuses and compensatory time are in order.

3. Consultants

Shake their hands, if appropriate. Make certain that they are paid, or make definite arrangements for payment. They are often considered overpaid, but many of them live on a small margin and don't have the security of the good old regular paycheck.

4. **Participants**

Specify dates for any materials to be provided (by you or them) later. Wave "bye."

5. **Structures**

In shambles.

6. **Aids**

Salvage the salvageable. Pack as well as possible. Record important data on the worksheet.

7. **Facility**

Take time to scrutinize the bill. It is difficult to make adjustments at a later date. Note any budget surprises on the worksheet. Pay the bill or make definite arrangements for payment. Distribute all gratuities! Be generous; you may want to come again.

8. **Accommodations**

Check out. Pay your own bill. Pay the bill for other accommodations covered by workshop budget or make definite payment arrangements. Make certain that staff hasn't "skipped the tab." Get your toothbrush.

9. **Food and Refreshments**

Provide payment and tips if still outstanding. Record any budget surprises.

10. **Dates**

You have a family to go home to.

11. **Travel**

I trust you've reconfirmed before now. Otherwise (particularly on Friday) check back into the hotel.

12. **Promotion**

Judge it either a failure or a success.

***   ***   ***

Return to center stage. Take a bow. Exit stage left, the sound of applause echoing in your ears.

CLOSING SHOP

Workshop   Date

1. Materials

Missing: _____
_____
_____
_____

2. Staff Debriefing

Significant Summations: _____
_____
_____
_____

3. Consultants

Payment Arrangements:
a) _____
b) _____
c) _____
d) _____

4. Participants:

Dates for materials: Items:
_____   _____
_____   _____
_____   _____
_____   _____

5. Structures: N/A

6. Aids

Significant items missing.
_____
_____
_____
_____

7. Facility

	paid	Date for payment
Bill: $_____	( )	_____
Tips: $_____	( )	
$_____	( )	
$_____	( )	

Budget surprises: Amt.

_____ $_____

_____ $_____

8. Accommodations

	paid	Date for payment
Bill $_____	( )	_____

9. Food & Refreshments

paid	Date for payment	Amt.	Tips
( )	_____	$_____	$_____
( )	_____	$_____	$_____
( )	_____	$_____	$_____

Budget surprises: Amt.

_____ $_____

_____ $_____

_____ $_____

10. Dates: N/A

11. Travel: N/A

12. Promotion: N/A

267

PART III

Evaluating
The Workshop

EVALUATING

Among theorists evaluation is one of the most hotly debated activities in the educational process; among practitioners it is one of the most ignored. This situation needs to be reversed. Theorists are primarily interested in evaluation as a means of proving the rightness of their theories; practitioners should be interested in evaluation as the only means of proving the success or failure of their workshops and their work.

In judging the success of any activity, you attempt to answer the question, "How did I do?" In judging the success of a workshop, there are two basic things to look for:

1. How did you do—in terms of meeting the learning objectives?

2. How did you do—in terms of participant reactions to the workshop work?

Evaluating the workshop also serves participant needs in at least three ways:

1. By requiring performance on the part of the participant, it serves to reinforce his learning.

271

2. By measuring performance against objectives, it lets the participant know if he has achieved the minimum competencies.

3. By measuring the distance between present performance and desired, it serves as a reassessment of participant needs.

Workshop evaluation is an activity that should occur during the course of the workshop, at the conclusion, and perhaps even later. During the workshop, evaluation provides data useful in making midcourse corrections. Evaluation at the conclusion of the workshop tells how you did and provides data useful in making future improvements. Evaluation after the workshop tells if the learning has held and if it is being used. Let's examine the four most common types of workshop evaluations, how and when to use them, and the advantages and disadvantages of each.

FEEDBACK FROM PARTICIPANTS

As traditionally used in educational circles, the word *feedback* describes data provided to the participant regarding the adequacy of his performance. It may take the form of scores, written or verbal critiques, or computer printouts. It most commonly refers to evaluation data provided the participant during the course of learning which assists him in correcting his errors or reinforces him in his correctness. The closer (in time) feedback is to performance, the more value it will have in correcting or reinforcing performance.

In modern adult education, feedback is often used to describe data provided by participants regarding the adequacy of the workshop and workshop staff performance. This reversal is the result of the recognition that adults have something to contribute to the learning. It assumes the value of their experience and their attitudes. As such, feedback from participants assists workshop staff in making corrections during the workshop itself or reinforces them in their correctness. Value is again related to timeliness.

Feedback from participants may be obtained in several ways.

1. Individual participants may be asked for their appraisal of the day's activities or some portion of them. This usually occurs during breaks, at the close of the session, or in the bar afterwards.

2. The entire group may be asked to provide written (often anonymous) appraisals of the day's activities or some portion of them. This often occurs at the close of the day's session. These comments are then reviewed by staff at the evening team meeting and hopefully used as guidance for the next day's events.

3. The entire group may be asked to provide verbal appraisals of the day's activities or some portion of them. This usually occurs right after some particular activity or at

the end of the day. It is accomplished by workshop staff coming offstage and getting down in the crowd.

4. When numbers make it impractical to receive feedback from all participants, a special feedback group can be formed for that purpose. This group usually provides their comments at the close of the session.

5. Since it provides instantaneous feedback, perhaps the most useful method is to invite participants to spontaneously offer comments in the course of the learning activities. This is the most adult method of feedback, and it requires a high level of trust. If this method is to be employed, the trust begins to grow with a stated invitation during the ground rules portion of climate setting and is reinforced by periodic "how am I doing's."

Feedback from participants has the advantage of giving data before it is too late. Its disadvantage lies in the fact that participants are often too polite. Specificity helps. For example, Worksheet 7 could be used by participants for written end-of-day feedback (the "Assignments" spaces would not apply).

POST-MEETING REACTION FORMATS

I often refer to these as "popularity polls." They normally take the form of a written reaction (often anonymous) provided by participants at the close of the workshop. Participants are usually happy at that point— at least to get it over with. Consequently they tend to give high marks that the workshop conductor can file in his portfolio or show to his boss whether or not the workshop was really worthwhile. Such formats range from open-ended questions to various rating scales. Participants are asked to evaluate such things as workshop organization, objectives, staff, facilities, and materials.

The popularity poll deficiency may be removed by comparing the results to established norms. The *Workshop Evaluation Scale* by Earl McCallon is an example of a normed scale based on reactions of over forty thousand participants in a variety of workshops. When using a normed scale, a rating that would normally be considered good may prove to be quite low when compared to the norm for the same element.

The advantage of post-meeting reaction formats are that they provide us with data useful in improving future workshops, and they are easily interpreted and administered, even if the group is large. Their disadvantage lies in the fact that participants are too nice.

EVALUATION BY OBJECTIVES

In both types of evaluation described above you determine participant reaction to the workshop. But how about the learning objectives? Did you reach them? Since workshops involve both content and process, both kinds of evaluations are essential.

275

Evaluation by objectives is the real payoff of this book. All the laborious activities of assessing needs, specifying objectives, designing learning activities to meet those objectives, etc., have been leading to this point. You may now measure the results. How? By simply having participants demonstrate the behavior described in the objective under the specified conditions, and by assessing their levels of performance against the standard also specified in the objective. That's all. You either reached the objective, or you did not. If not, you have before you a completed needs assessment for future learning activities and a ticket back to the drawing board. If you did reach the objective, you can *prove* your success for anyone who is interested, and participants feel secure in the knowledge of their new competency.

This type of evaluation can take any form, so long as it realistically measures the learning outcome. In the chapter "Specifying Objectives," there is a warning. Let me repeat it: **The evaluation should simulate or approximate the way the behavior will be used in real life.** Written tests should be used for evaluation only when the real life performance involves writing in exactly the same way. These evaluations more typically take the form of case studies, role plays, and other activities. Check the "Methods Primer" for ideas.

Because the methods involved in evaluation by objective are active and flexible, this type of evaluation can provide feedback to the participants during the course of the workshop. It may also be used to evaluate participants at the end. Each SLO can be measured, step by step; participants can try out the behavior, receive feedback, and try again until they succeed. The objectives may also be used as a means for checking learning "fade" at some specified period(s) after the workshop. Used in this way, they serve to further reinforce the learning.

276

In the course of helping adult educators develop competencies, I have encountered two curious responses to this type of evaluation. Some feel uncomfortable asking participants to demonstrate their competencies. This is normally the result of something forced in either the needs assessment activity or in the contracting activity. In discussing their feelings, these educators usually admit that the learning has been imposed, and their discomfort comes from the fact that the evaluation would also be an imposition. **Evaluation by objectives is not an imposition on adults when they have freely "contracted" on the objectives.**

The other response is from educators who have been exposed to graduate school scientism. These educators have a strong need for scientific measurements, for pre- and post-testing, control groups and the like. Aside from the near impossibility of achieving adequate controls and the expense and time involved, I have no objection to this kind of precision, but it simply isn't needed in the daily practice of adult education. The kind of needs assessment described in this book does quite nicely as a pretest. The negotiated process involved therein is better than certified scores for producing both management and participant commitment to meeting the need. The demonstrated new behaviors are their own proof, and control groups only serve to tell (after the fact) whether the need was met by the workshop or some other factors. That kind of hindsight is not very useful when you are continuously confronted by new problems. While waiting for the academician to crank out his report, the practitioner might just as well proceed to look for solutions to the new problems using the crude tools of eyes and ears. However it occurs, the new competency is the point, not the proof of its parentage.

The major disadvantage to this type of evaluation is the difficulty in conducting it with large groups. With large groups it is difficult to measure meaningful learning at all. In that case, you might do better to simply use normed reaction scales and skip the evaluation of learning.

IMPACT EVALUATION

This type of evaluation attempts to measure the impact of the workshop on participant behavior back on the job and consequently, the impact on the organization itself. Again the difficulty is in isolating the variables, which often include many of the nonlearning needs described earlier. Without substantial and perhaps impossible controls, this kind of evaluation tells only that the behavior did or did not occur, not how it occurred. A lack of application or transfer may be the result of an unsupportive job environment rather than a lack of learning. Use this type of evaluation only when you can assure that all other variables are controlled. That is practically never. When attempted, it works something like this:

1. A selected behavior is measured prior to the workshop.

2. A prediction is made of what the workshop might change.

3. Other variables are monitored for their potential impact.

4. The selected behavior is again measured after the workshop using the same measurement tool.

The procedure described above measures impact from some source on individual behavior. You may use the same procedure to measure organizational impact by simply selecting an organizational indicator (e.g., absentee rate, complaints) to replace the behavior.

The disadvantages of this type of evaluation are obvious; advantages are questionable. It tells only how employees are behaving and it is very expensive.

OTHER (NONLEARNING) EVALUATIONS

Since evaluation types and uses are so often confused, I have included two nonlearning types for the sake of clarity.

1. *Organizational evaluations*—measure an entire organization's progress toward pre-established goals and objectives. This may also apply to divisions within an organization.

2. *Job performance evaluations* — measure what an employee actually does on the job. Performance is preferably measured against pre-established objectives that coincide with the organization's objectives and are stated in very specific terms. (A competency model can be used as the basis for these objectives.)

SUMMARY

Participant reaction evaluations help improve workshops. Evaluations based on objectives tell what a participant *can do* at the conclusion of a workshop. Impact evaluations require the control of all other variables. Job performance evaluations, rather than impact evaluations, are best for purposes of measuring what the participant *actually does* back on the job. If learning evaluations prove that a participant *can do* something, the workshop has met its responsibility. The actual doing is the responsibility of the participant and his boss.

STYLE VARIATIONS

Extreme authoritarian—Tends to give written tests that prove no more than participant subservience. Would not think of having participants evaluate him in return.

Extreme laissez faire—Feels that evaluations are invasions of privacy. The participant knows best.

Moderate authoritarian—Rigorously measures the results against objectives, whether participants agree to the objectives or not.

Moderate laissez faire—Assists participants in evaluating themselves in rather general ways. Seeks to be evaluated by participants.

Democratic—Measures the minimum required results against mutually agreeable objectives as the main means of judging workshop success. Seeks participant reaction as a means of improving workshops.

***   ***   ***

Worksheet 9 follows on the next page. It may be used for recording the results of several evaluations against objectives. The vertical column on the left has spaces for recording the names of eight participants. The spaces below GLO's and the numbered SLO's may be used for describing the learning being measured.

The rating scale is the same one used for competency model needs assessment. The "Rating" space is for the numerical rating. "Tips" may be one or two words that suggest needed improvements. The average of individual ratings provides a group rating. The "Summary Comments" column is for narrative summations of individual and group performance.

Workshop: _____ **Dates:** _____

EVALUATION BY OBJECTIVES
(By Individual)
COMPETENCY RATING SCALE

Inadequate —3, —2, —1   Adequate +1, +2, +3

GLO: _____

GROUP NAME: _____

Participant Names		SLO #1	SLO #2	SLO #3	SLO #4	SLO #5	SLO #6	SLO #7	SLO #8	SUMMARY COMMENTS
	Group Average									Group Comments:
1.	Rating									Participant Comments
	Tips									1.
2.	Rating									
	Tips									2.
3.	Rating									
	Tips									3.
4.	Rating									
	Tips									4.
5.	Rating									
	Tips									5.
6.	Rating									
	Tips									6.
7.	Rating									
	Tips									7.
8.	Rating									
	Tips									8.

282

Further Resources

NOTES

1. Tielhard de Chardin, Pierre, *The Phenomenon of Man*, p. 64.

2. Odiorne, George S., *Training by Objectives*, p. 149.

3. Mager, Robert F., *Developing Attitude Toward Learning*, p. 14.

4. Knowles, Malcolm S. and Hulda, *Introduction to Group Dynamics*, pp. 39-40.

5. Knowles, Malcolm S., *The Modern Practice of Adult Education*, p. 65 (adapted).

BIBLIOGRAPHY

Berne, Eric. *Games People Play*. New York: Grove Press, 1964.

Knowles, Malcolm S. *The Adult Learner: A Neglected Species*. Houston: Gulf Publishing Co., 1973.

_____. *The Modern Practice of Adult Education*. New York: Association Press, 1970.

Knowles, Malcolm S. and Hulda. *Introduction to Group Dynamics*. New York: Association Press, 1959.

Lippit, Gordon L. *Organizational Renewal*. New York: Appleton-Century-Crofts, 1969.

Mager, Robert F. *Developing Attitude Toward Learning*. Belmont, Calif.: Fearon Publishers, 1968.

_____. *Preparing Instructional Objectives*. Belmont, Calif.: Fearon Publishers, 1962.

Margolis, Fredric H. *Training By Objectives*. Cambridge, Mass: McBer and Company, 1970.

Mills, H. R. *Teaching and Training—A Handbook for Instructors*. New York: John Wiley & Sons, n.d. (1972).

Odiorne, George S. *Training by Objectives*. London: Macmillan, 1970.

Rogers, Carl R. *Client-Centered Therapy*. Boston: Houghton Mifflin Co., 1965.

Skinner, B. F. *Beyond Freedom and Dignity*. New York: Alfred E. Knopf, 1971.

_____. *The Technology of Teaching*. New York: Appleton-Century-Crofts, 1968.

_____. *Walden Two*. New York: McMillan, 1962.

Teilhard de Chardin, Pierre. *The Phenomenon of Man*. New York: Harper & Row, 1959.

Toffler, Alvin. *Future Shock*. New York: Random House, 1970.

AMERICAN SOCIETY FOR TRAINING AND
DEVELOPMENT
P. O. Box 5307
Madison, Wisconsin 53705

You may be interested in membership in ASTD, the national professional organization for trainers.

This organization publishes a monthly journal, conducts periodic seminars for its members and sponsors an annual conference. There are local ASTD chapters in several major cities.

A

MANAGER'S GUIDE

TO

STAFF DEVELOPMENT

STAFF DEVELOPMENT IN YOUR ORGANIZATION

The Unwanted Child

For starters, let's agree that staff development is somewhat like an unwanted child—often abused, sometimes neglected, perhaps pacified, but seldom loved. You see the parallel. Let's take the analogy further. Like the unwanted child, staff development was conceived by rather vague organizational planning, was carried in a climate of crisis, and delivered into a world of conflicting expectations and emotions. And on top of all that, it behaved rather badly.

If you agree with the above, then clearly we either need to stop staff development or do it better. But before we reach a decision, perhaps it would be prudent to analyze (a good management practice) why it happened wrong in the first place.

What Went Wrong

For purposes of this analysis, we will not explore the child's bad behavior. This is the subject of training for staff developers. Instead we will be interested in what the parents (managers) were up to. As we all know, managers come in a variety of styles, and similarly, their ways of fostering unwanted children also vary. Let's examine a few:

293

FIRST

In the midst of innocent excitement, managers, coping with their normal daily crises, let loose the idea that some training might help. After expressing surprise and claiming a virgin birth, they sent the wondrous child into the world to work miracles—turning darkness into light, pain into pleasure, discord into harmony. Little wonder that the poor kid was crucified.

ANOTHER

From the godfather role, managers, seeking a way to impose their ways of doing things, made a persuasive offer in the form of "someone needs to motivate those people to do their jobs right" or some such phrase. And they sent the subservient but bossy child out to do his parents' bidding. And behold, those perverse and ungrateful employees sat in grim silence or rose in rebellion.

AND FINALLY

Since everybody else is doing it, managers, not really seeing the point, sent the rather bored and droning child out under the banner of "We've Got to Keep Pace." These managers, expect-

ing nothing to happen, proved themselves right.

Does the picture look bleak? Well, perhaps better
information would have yielded more fruitful planning
and a different outcome. So let's take a look at what
these managers should have known about staff development activities.

Staff Development as a Management Aid

Perhaps most important, a manager needs to know
what training can do for his organization—and what it
cannot do. It can, for instance, help an organization
reach its goals; it cannot solve all of the organization's
problems. It can help individual employees increase their
knowledge and skill; it can help them develop new and
happier attitudes; it cannot make up for an inadequate
salary. It can help employees learn how to use good management systems; it cannot smooth over bad ones. And
it cannot motivate employees to function effectively
under inept or oppressive management.

Managers also need to know that training is an activity that involves not only the *content* to be learned,
but the *process* of learning it. It is not enough to have an
employee exposed to accurate and expert information.
The information must be "experienced" in order to take.
A spirited presentation may be entertaining, and an
authoritative one may receive respect, but they do not
necessarily result in learning. Learning occurs when the
process of inquiry (or practice) is appropriately designed.

And finally, managers need to understand that
learning is a growth process. It is not, at least primarily,
treatment for a sick organization; it is food for a healthy

295

one. And like any other growth process, the cessation of it is followed by stagnation and decay.

Let's look at this information in more detail.

How Adults Learn

It can be argued that in learning situations adults are different from children in many respects. To be sure, such an argument depends on generalization. Some children react very maturely, and some adults very childishly. Nonetheless, such generalizations form the basis for adult education practices that often make the difference between effective and ineffective staff development programs. Too often educational practices traditionally associated with children are applied to adults. Let's explore a few of the more crucial generalizations and the implications they have for adult learning activities.

1. Adults have a good deal of first hand experience. As a result they know or think they know a good deal about the content of their experience. Educational activities that ignore that experience are often seen as insulting. Educational activities that build on it are usually received with enthusiasm. Educational activities that tap that experience as a contribution to the learning of others frequently find a valuable resource.

2. Adults have a great many preoccupations outside of a particular learning situation. They have fam-

ilies to feed, children to care for, and social obligations. And they want to get on with their work. Educational activities that waste adults' time are usually wasted. Educational activities that honor and protect their time receive the attention they deserve.

3. Adults have real decisions to make and real problems to solve. Educational activities that amble around in abstractions unrelated to these decisions and problems tend to be lost on adults. Educational activities that assist adults in making necessary decisions and solving pressing problems tend to be closely followed. The basics of a subject are quite often unessential; adults need information and skills relevant to current problems and decisions.

4. Adults exhibit habitual responses to authority. Some buck it, some bow to it. Some relate to it as a necessary evil, and a few relate to it as a needed resource. Educational activities deriving their justification from authority may be resisted either actively or passively. Adults may either refuse to cooperate or appear to go along while simply avoiding learning. When tests are

involved, adults may learn but not change their practices back on the job.

5. Adults have a certain amount of pride and prefer to be self-directed whenever possible. Educational activities that derive their justification at least partially from self-stated participant needs tend to receive willing acceptance and serious efforts to learn.

6. Adults have real things to lose. They are prone to avoid active participation in educational activities when they feel that the demonstration of any inadequacy might lead to unfavorable personnel actions. They resist learning that may be unpopular back in the shop, and they are not likely to apply learning that goes unrewarded.

An Organizational Climate That Enhances Learning

Just as cell reproduction is a growth process that occurs best under certain conditions, learning is a growth process that is strongly affected by its environment. If that environment happens to be a group organized for the purpose of accomplishing work, the climate in which learning occurs is largely the product of the organization's management. That climate can be favorable or unfavorable.

The preceding comments concerning adult learning suggest that the most favorable climate for staff development is one in which employees are respected, their experience is valued, their ideas used, and their problems taken seriously. This implies the presence of management styles and procedures that encourage participation, a total management approach which allows all employees "ownership" in the organization's work.

The Professional Staff Developer

Given a favorable climate, adults usually need the help of a professional adult educator (trainer) to learn effectively. The professional trainer is one who has a working knowledge of the *process* of adult learning and who has mastered the art and skill of designing and conducting learning experiences appropriate to adults.

In this field, content expertise is most often supplied by supervisors, the learning group itself, or other resources, such as written materials or visiting specialists. The trainer's expertise is in designing a series of learning experiences that lead to learning objectives and in helping learners achieve their objectives.

Applying this to your organization, if you are going to initiate a staff development program, you need to hire such a person or select someone from your staff who will prepare for the specialized discipline described above. If selecting someone already in your organization you should look for two qualities: 1) a strong sense of self-confidence that holds up even in unknown situations and 2) the ability to give and receive constructive criticism.

The Staff Developer's Tool Kit

The staff developer needs a good supply of integrity, patience, ink markers, ears, eyes, and newsprint. He needs a well-oiled voice and a free-swinging body. He needs courage and the self-confidence to say, "I don't know." Most of all he needs to know how to behave himself in a systematic series of activities that lead to effective adult learning.

Following is a brief description of those activities. The sequence presented here is the normal one, though it may sometimes vary slightly.

1. *Assessing Needs*

There are only two basic ways of assessing needs. Each has variations.

The first way is to start with a problem, any problem. A valiant effort is made to find the real problem behind the apparent problem. This done, the problem is translated into a series of statements that describe what *needs* to happen to solve it. These are then separated into needs that can be met by someone's learning something and needs that must be met some other way. The ones that involve learning are prioritized, and if sufficient commitment exists, carted back to the trainer's drawing board to be converted into objectives.

The second way is to develop a competency model. This is simply a series of statements that describe what a good "something" (i.e., supervisor) does and how he does it. With the aid of other input, the prospective trainees then assess themselves against the model and tell the trainer what they need to learn to reach the ideal of the model. These needs are prioritized for group learning, and if sufficient commitment exists, are carted off to the drawing board.

Either way, the main point is that the prospective learner participates in identifying his own needs. In practice, this involves a negotiated agreement between employees, management, and the trainer.

2. Specifying Learning Objectives

This is something the staff developer usually does alone, since it requires a precise technical skill. The agreed-upon needs are converted into a number of learning objectives. Each objective (Specific Learning Objective) should be very precise. It should address only one of the three types of learning—knowledge learning, skill learning, or attitude learning.

It should also describe the means of seeing if the objective has been reached. This is done by stating: 1) the observable behavior the learner will perform, 2) the level of acceptable performance, and 3) the conditions under which he will perform.

3. Selecting Resources for Learning

In this activity the staff developer tentatively selects materials and people who may contribute to the learning. He attempts to select resources that are the best available for meeting the objectives. The resources should also conform to his educational style and to the participants' expectations.

4. Designing Learning Activities

This again is the staff developer's job. With lots of resource materials and a bit of divine inspiration, he plans a series of learning experiences that lead to

301

and include the learner's demonstration that the objective has been reached.

5. *Budgeting*

Given the selected resources and design decisions, the staff developer now prepares a detailed budget to see what he can afford. If necessary, he considers alternatives and makes revisions.

6. *Making Arrangements*

Budget in hand, the staff developer begins to arrange the multiplicity of details that contribute to effective learning activities. These include arrangements for materials, staff, consultants, equipment, facilities, and travel, to name only a few. On the basis of this data, a firm date is set and the workshop is advertised.

7. *Rehearsing*

Like a Broadway cast, everything is rehearsed. Problems are ironed out, and the production is polished.

8. *Packing*

The staff developer, not a secretary, makes certain that everything is present, accounted for, and sent packing to the learning site. When satisfied, he checks to see if he has his toothbrush.

9. *Setting Up*

Everything is unpacked, checked, and placed. Facility arrangements are rechecked, the staff meets for final instructions, and the workshop is pronounced "GO."

10. *Setting the Climate for Learning*

This is the first thing that happens in the session itself. Assuming that the management-induced climate is conducive for learning, the trainer greets participants, proposes ground rules which describe how he and the trainees will relate during the learning process, leads everyone in a warm-up, and makes certain that all expectations are focused in the same direction.

11. *Agreeing on Objectives*

Expectations vibrating in harmony, the staff developer reminds everyone of the needs that brought them together. He provides an opportunity for participants to explore the proposed objectives to see if they faithfully respond to the agreed-upon needs. Suggested modifications are discussed and appropriate changes made. He "closes the deal" with a contract between himself and participants, binding them together in mutual pursuit of the objectives.

12. *Directing Learning Activities*

Displaying an amazing range of behaviors, the staff developer leads, assists, and directs participants through a designed series of learning activities. He is sensitive to the need for changing planned activities and is quick in making necessary changes.

13. *Closing Shop*

Finishing touches include packing the remnants and paying the bills.

14. *Evaluating Learning Activities*

This activity is listed last because it is the final phase of the closed-loop system that returns the staff developer to the needs assessment step. In practice, evaluation may occur during, at the conclusion of, or sometime after the workshop.

Very simply, the learner observably performs as described in the objective, and he and the staff developer evaluate his performance against the standard agreed upon in the objectives. In addition to measuring the results of the workshop, the evaluation serves as a reinforcement of learning and a reassessment of needs.

The process is again at the beginning!

What Managers Do in Staff Development

First, let's look at this in the light of the process described above.

1. *Needs Assessment*

Management calls for needs assessment. After the staff developer and employees have identified needs, management reviews them, suggests modifications, and endorses a negotiated and prioritized list to be addressed in training.

2. *Learning Objectives*

   Management should check them for precision and
   agree to the validity of the "test" (is the performance the same as or similar to that which will be required on the job).

3. *Resource Selection*

   Management should review the tentative selections,
   suggest modifications if necessary, and approve continuation of the planning process.

4. *Learning Design*

   Management may review the finished design but
   should yield to the staff developer's professional
   judgement.

5. *Budget*

   Management provides an operating budget and may
   authorize expenditures for particular learning activities. Management encourages comptroller cooperation.

6. *Arrangements*

   Management may make suggestions but should
   defer to staff developer's decisions for the sake of
   effective learning. Management assists staff devel
   oper in arranging for additional in-house staff.

7. *Rehearsal*

   Management should stay well away.

8. *Packing*

Management should avoid involvement.

9. *Set-up*

Management attending workshop might buy the staff developer a drink.

10. *Learning climate (in session)*

Management good will should be felt, but management's physical absence should be noted, unless they are part of the workshop staff or are full participants in the learning activities.

11. *Goal Agreement*

Management authorizes staff developer to negotiate any necessary changes.

12. *Learning Sessions*

Management, if present, should participate fully or find something else to do. Management should avoid taking over.

13. *Close*

Management provides assurance to hotel management that bills will be paid.

14. *Evaluation*

When learning activities are completed, including any necessary reruns, management should review tne results with the staff developer to make certain that standards were applied equally to all. Now management knows what employees *can* do. What they actually do is management's problem and can be determined with job performance evaluation.

In addition to the participation in the process itself, managers need to lend some additional support. They should authorize, recognize, and announce the staff developer's professional status. They need to make paid time available to staff for training, and they need to back up the training effort with required resources. Getting down to the nitty-gritty, they need to spell all this out in an agency policy statement on staff development. That statement should address the following ten points:

Content of Agency Policy

Good staff development must be undergirded by a strong agency policy statement. Such statements should:

1. Clearly relate staff development to accomplishment of the organization's objectives;

2. Explicitly state a philosophical commitment to the value of human growth and individual fulfillment;

3. Clearly describe how training needs within the organization will be identified;

4. Explicitly state that training needs identified will *not* be used to jeopardize an employee's job security;

5. Explicitly state that changes in employment status must result from evaluation of job performance and not evaluation of performance in training activities;

6. Clearly identify the resources committed to staff development just as they are identified for other organizational functions (e.g., funds, time, space, manpower, materials, and equipment);

7. Clearly specify the relationship of the staff development component to other organizational components and specify individual responsibilities for each step in the staff development process within those components;

8. Specify who will be served in staff development activities;

9. Specify general parameters and any limitations placed on the scope of staff development activities;

10. Clearly describe and authorize relationships to other institutions which might further staff development efforts.[5]

And finally, for the usual reasons, management should press for and bless a long-range (as opposed to crises) staff development plan.

Even When It's Planned

Even when staff development is a planned child, a few potential problems remain:

1. *The balance of on-job time with training time.*

   Even when things are going well, new learning is needed, but it should not undercut your present productivity. Neither should sloppy habits and outmoded practices be allowed to continue.

2. *The problem of bringing problems out in the open*

   This will arise most often in the problem-analysis method of needs assessment. In an organization where everyone really has ownership, this is no problem. But if you are coming on like a dictator, beware of a revolutionary fever.

3. *Organizational goals versus individual goals.*

   Finally, it is possible for staff development to become too responsive to the individual. Employees are there to do a job, and the organization's goals come first.

Decision Time

Now that the information has been reviewed, it is up to you, the manager, to make the free choice of improving your staff development activities or stopping them.

ABOUT THE AUTHOR

Larry Davis has been "on the line" in training and consultation for more than thirteen years. He came to the training
field via a circuitous route (as do most trainers) starting with
writing the great American novel in a loft in New York City.
The novel went into a trunk, but his writer's curiosity about
people and what makes them tick (or helps them learn) remains.
Larry's first experiences in the training field were in government, the U.S. Post Office and the fledgling Office of Economic
Opportunity. He soon became adept at cutting red tape and
working in and around bureaucracies. That led to a variety of
experiences as a free-lance consultant to government, private
associations, industry, and education. Larry learned first-
hand the differences between no-budget training and unlimited
funds; the importance and nuances of authority in training;
the training methods most likely to result in a good workshop.
By necessity, he created a great many of the systems detailed
in this book. Continuing experiences in settings ranging from
management training to child development allowed him to
refine, distill, and reassess the approach to training offered in
this book. In recent years, Larry has specialized in learning
systems and trainer-training. As readers, you are spared the
painfulness of walking "on the line" for the first time and
instead are offered the comfort of trying on some well-worn
boots.

Larry currently stomps around Texas and the rest of the
world offering professional consultation through his firm,
Larry Davis and Associates of Austin, Texas.